1% WARRIOR™
BLACK BELT BOSS

A.J. Madden

This book is dedicated to my brother Michael, my longest and best training partner and friend.

Table of Contents

Introduction 7
Billionaires and Black Belts 12
Simplicity and Narrow Focus, Big Vision and Living Limitless:
Bruce Lee and Steve Jobs.. 13
Guiding Philosophy: Miyamoto Musashi and Jeff Bezos 17
Incredible Self Belief and Growth Mindset: Conor McGregor
and Kanye West 23
Work Ethic and Daily Routine: Jocko Willink and Elon Musk.... 26
Deep Learning: Georges St. Pierre and Warren Buffett 30
15 Lessons For A New Martial Artist And Leader..................... 34

SELF PROTECTION PILLAR ONE:
AWARENESS AND AVOIDANCE 41
   PRINCIPLE #1: Be Your Own Protector 42
   PRINCIPLE #2: Don't Be There 44
   PRINCIPLE #3: Sheepdog Mentality 47

SELF PROTECTION PILLAR TWO: ATTITUDE 50
   PRINCIPLE #4: Attitude Is A Weapon 51
   PRINCIPLE #5: Never See Yourself On The Losing Side Of Violence . 54
   PRINCIPLE #6: Mental, Emotional, and Physical Posture 56
   PRINCIPLE #7: The Power Of No 58
   PRINCIPLE #8: Capable Of Cruelty....................................... 60
   PRINCIPLE #9: Do The Single Hardest Thing...................... 63
   PRINCIPLE #10: Let People Keep Their Dignity 66
   PRINCIPLE #11: Always Trust Your Gut 71

SELF PROTECTION PILLAR THREE: ANIMAL 73
    PRINCIPLE #12:   Fitness Is A Weapon 75
    PRINCIPLE #13:   Golden Moves 81
    PRINCIPLE #14:   Don't Step Back Psychology 85
    PRINCIPLE #15:   Hit Three Times Harder (Force Multipliers)............ 88
    PRINCIPLE #16:   The BEST Defense 97
    PRINCIPLE #17:   The Water Balloon And The Ice Sculpture 101
    PRINCIPLE #18:   Splatter Factor 104
    PRINCIPLE #19:   No Guarantees 108
    PRINCIPLE #20:   Keep Showing Up (Keep Training) 111
    PRINCIPLE #21:   Iron Sharpens Iron (Find The Best People) 116
    PRINCIPLE #22:   Ten Minutes With A Mentor.................................. 119
    PRINCIPLE #23:   Weaponize Your Instincts 122
    PRINCIPLE #24:   White Belt Mentality (Never Stop Learning)........ 125

Conclusion: Don't Be There 128
24 Principles Of Self Protection Summaries 131
Recommended Books, Films and Documentaries, and
YouTube Channels 167
About The Author 172

Introduction

> *"Confidence applied properly surpasses genius."*
> *- Mike Tyson*

Leadership is the answer.

Confidence is a vital function of leadership.

Don't overthink this.

It's not that complicated

Looking back, every major problem or failure in my life was caused by fear and a lack of confidence.

Through training in self defense and mixed martial arts, you will improve your what I call "physical confidence". When your physical confidence improves, increased mental confidence will naturally follow. The mind and body are inextricably connected.

My definition of a "Black Belt Boss":

A person who's life is fully committed to becoming the best leader they can possibly be in service of others.

My Story

My training and leadership journey began at age 12. My father, in his wisdom, got me a weight training set. I received one of my most important life lessons:

Confidence comes through repetition. Repetition leads to growth and improvement. Growth and improvement lead to confidence.

Additionally at age 12, my uncle James Madden began teaching me about business. He took me to Boston to see how one of his company stores was built. He was an integral part in building the company into a multi-billion-dollar corporation that had stores in all fifty states and on four continents. He passed many business and leadership lessons on to me over the next three decades.

A few years later in 1994, another very important thing in my life happened. The second UFC event showed up on the shelf at my local video store. I rented it over and over again. I was fascinated by the efficiency and effectiveness of the Brazilian Jiu Jitsu of the undersized champion Royce Gracie.

It would take another ten years for me to begin MMA training, as mixed martial arts was still in its infancy stages and the training opportunities were very limited outside of larger cities and small pockets across the country.

At age 23, I received my philosophy degree from Bloomburg University. It was another key moment, as my philosophy study taught me one of the most important lessons in life: never stop learning.

At age 25, I began reading all of the best of the best books I could find on leadership, business, and personal development. This opened my eyes to a whole new world of possibilities.

Coinciding with the deep reading and learning, I began my mixed martial arts and self defense training in State College, PA under Sensei's Dave Light and Cory Wimberly, and Jeremy Corbell at

Quantum Jiu Jitsu, and Bruce Lombard at Titan Fitness and Lombard MMA. I can easily say it was one of the best decisions I've ever made. I have now been fortunate to train in 16 different martial arts, with multiple national and world champion fighters, and have learned directly from some of the most respected self defense instructors on the planet.

There's a saying coined by the legendary Brazilian Jiu Jitsu black belt Chris Haughter:

"It's not who's good, it's who's left."

I just kept showing up. It's that simple.

When you train with high level amateur and professional cage fighters, boxers, wrestlers, and kickboxers, you understand there are levels to the game. You learn a healthy respect for the capabilities of a human being when they are well trained in the arts of hand to hand combat. I learned a ton from the following fighters and combat athletes: my brother Mike Madden, my father Al Madden, my cousins Michael Matthew and Matt, my uncle Mike, Richard Brooks, Ethan Goss, Tom Hanelly, Jon Marsh, Tyler Saltsman, Shawn Slater, Mike Putnam, Tyler Higgins, Os Omo-Osagie, Corey Tilghman, Whitney Pequignot, Ariel Webb, CP Prasad, Dan Radnor, Jeremy Guillard, Brad Struble, Anthony Colonna, Jake Strickler, Sam Meyer, Dylan Short, and Mory Diané.

By working with and training with people of this caliber, you learn one of the most important lessons of leadership: respect and humility.

Around the same time I started mma training, I started working as a bouncer, bartender, and eventually general manager of a multi-million dollar nightclub.

The nightclubs served as a laboratory and training ground for me in three crucial areas:

Leadership

Business

And reality-based self defense.

The nightclub was a high speed, fast paced, pressure testing, and low margin for error "laboratory" to test out all of the "best practices" I had been deeply studying.

I learned countless lessons in the nightclubs. Many of those will shared in this book.

Around the age of 25, I came to the conclusion that:

1. If I studied and learned the high-level habits and mindsets of the best leaders of today and throughout history, and
2. If I put those habits and mindsets into practice, then
3. I would be valuable to any and every organization on the planet and I would never go hungry.

Because every problem is a leadership problem. And every solution is a leadership solution.

So I kept up with my continuous self-education going for the next 15 years.

I saw two interesting statistics many years ago on the two wealthiest men in America at the time. The best part about them is, anyone can do it if they commit to it:

Bill Gates worked ten years straight without a vacation to build Microsoft

Warren Buffett reads 5-6 hours a day.

I made the decision to do both.

I have worked for ten-years plus without a vacation, trying to improve my leadership and self defense knowledge and abilities.

During those years, I read and listened to educational materials for 5-6 hours a day.

Between those ten years plus the ten years before, I have now spent around 40,000 hours plus of study, practice and teaching the mindsets and habits of peak performance, martial arts, and leadership.

They were at the bar.

I was at Barnes and Noble.

The average American watches 5 hours of TV a day.

I took in 5 hours a day or more of educational material.

This is what it takes.

Here we are today.

This book is the distilled lessons learned in the last twenty years.

I hope you find it useful.

Billionaires and Black Belts

> *"A person's paradigm produces their results. You will find that everyone who has done anything of consequence is totally illogical relative to the masses."*
>
> -Bob Proctor

There are some fascinating similarities between some of the most successful business leaders on the planet, and some of the greatest martial artists of all time.

We'll take an in-depth look at five case study comparisons and discuss the success principles that drive their best-in-class performance and achievement:

1. Simplicity and Narrow Focus, Big Vision and Living Limitless: Bruce Lee and Steve Jobs
2. Simple Guiding Philosophy: Miyamoto Musashi and Jeff Bezos
3. Incredible Self Belief and Growth Mindset: Conor McGregor and Kanye West
4. Work Ethic and Daily Routine: Jocko Willink and Elon Musk
5. Deep Learning: Georges St. Pierre and Warren Buffett

These traits and principles are fundamentals of success and great leadership. We'll now take a look at the processes used by some of the greatest visionaries of the last century, explained in their own words.

Simplicity and Narrow Focus, Big Vision and Living Limitless: Bruce Lee and Steve Jobs

> *"You are what you think. Elite performers think on an elite level."*
> —Troy Bassham

Both Steve Jobs and Bruce Lee were driven by what would appear to be diametrically opposing concepts. Narrow focus. And living limitless with a big vision. However, one of the secrets of success is being able to hold to seemingly opposing concepts in your head at the same time.

You *can* think big and focus small.

Simplicity and Narrow Focus

Steve Jobs believed, "The only thing that differentiated me was my level of focus."

Bruce Lee surmised, "Concentration is the ROOT of all the higher abilities in man."

Steve lived his life in the pursuit of simplicity and focus. In his own words:

"That's been one of my mantras — focus and simplicity. Simple can be harder than complex: You have to work hard to get your thinking clean to make it simple. But it's worth it in the end because once you get there, you can move mountains."

"I know you have 1000 great ideas for things that iTunes could do. And we have 1000 more. But innovation is not about saying "yes" to everything. It's about saying "no" to all but the most crucial features."

Bruce had a philosophy of reductionism that permeated his life and martial arts:

"Adapt what is useful, reject what is useless, and add what is specifically your own."

"It is not the daily increase, but the daily decrease. Hack away at the inessentials."

"Genius: The capacity to see an express what is simple, simply!"

"I fear not the man who has practiced 10,000 kicks once, but I fear the man who has practiced one kick 10,000 times."

Big Vision

Steve wanted to "put a dent in the universe". It doesn't get much bigger than that.

Bruce was a student of the works of Napoleon Hill, including his classic book "Think And Grow Rich".

> *"All success begins with definiteness of purpose, with a clear picture in your mind of precisely what you want in life."*
>
> *-Napoleon Hill*

Bruce created his mission statement, or what Hill called a "Definite Chief Aim" and wrote it out in 1969 at the age of 28:

My Definite Chief Aim

I, Bruce Lee, will be the first highest paid Oriental super star in the United States. In return I will give the most exciting performances and render the best of quality in the capacity of an actor. Starting 1970 I will achieve world fame and from then onward till the end of 1980 I will have in my possession $10,000,000. I will live the way I please and achieve inner harmony and happiness.

Bruce Lee

Jan. 1969

Bruce understood the power of having a big vision.

Living Limitless

According to his biographer Walter Isaacson, "Steve Jobs believed in the power of the will to bend reality."

Bruce believed in living limitless:

"If you always put limits on everything you do, physical or anything else, it will spread into your work and into your life. There are no limits."

Andy Cunningham, Steve's publicist, described a "reality distortion field":

"Steve Jobs often used the phrase reality distortion field. Others used it to describe the environment in which he operated. It applies to a number of ways that Steve behaved. The first and foremost way is that it was all about his belief that the impossible was possible. When you worked with Steve Jobs, everything that seemed impossible, he made possible or he made you make it possible."

Bruce talked about his own "force":

"As long as I can remember I feel I have had this great creative and spiritual force within me that is greater than faith, greater than ambition, greater than confidence, greater than determination, greater than vision. It is all these combined. My brain becomes magnetized with this dominating force which I hold in my hand."

Steve Jobs and Bruce Lee both exemplified simplicity, while at the same time living limitless. Through this, they both were able put their own dent in the universe and impact the lives of millions.

Guiding Philosophy: Miyamoto Musashi and Jeff Bezos

> *"There is nothing outside of yourself that can ever enable you to get better, stronger, richer, quicker, or smarter. Everything is within. Everything exists. Seek nothing outside of yourself."*
>
> -Miyamoto Musashi

Legendary samurai Miyamoto Musashi and Jeff Bezos, the wealthiest man in America, both had simple guiding philosophies that fueled their accomplishments.

Musashi was a Japanese swordsman, philosopher, and author of "The Book of Five Rings" and Dokkōdō (The Path of Aloneness). He was a military strategist and ronin (wandering samurai).

Musashi, had an undefeated record in his 61 duels, and is known as the greatest samurai. He is one of the few individuals to be regarded as a Kensei, a sword-saint of Japan.

He lived a solitary, Monk-like, tightly disciplined existence.

In his book Dokkodo (The Way of Aloneness), he wrote about 21 principles to guide one's life.

21 Rules To Live Your Life By

1. Accept everything just the way it is
2. Do not seek pleasure for its own sake

3. Do not, under any circumstances, depend on a partial feeling
4. Think lightly of yourself and deeply of the world
5. Be detached from desire your whole life long
6. Do not regret what you have done
7. Never be jealous
8. Never let yourself be saddened by a separation
9. Resentment and complaint are appropriate neither for oneself or others
10. Do not let yourself be guided by the feeling of lust or love
11. In all things have no preferences
12. Be indifferent to where you live
13. Do not pursue the taste of good food
14. Do not hold on to possessions you no longer need
15. Do not act following customary beliefs
16. Do not collect weapons or practice with weapons beyond what is useful
17. Do not fear death
18. Do not seek to possess either goods or fiefs for your old age
19. Respect Buddha and the gods without counting on their help
20. You may abandon your own body but you must preserve your honour
21. Never stray from the Way

Jeffrey Preston Bezos is the CEO, and president, and founder of the multi-national technology company Amazon.

Bezos deeply believes in the importance of core values and principles when running a business. They are applied to Amazon's day-to-day business operations, as well as to any new business ventures and expansions. Their core values are a common thread that runs through the company's history.

Bezos used the following "14 Leadership Principles" to build a trillion dollar company.

These principles are used in the company's daily language and practice for all employees and leaders.

The 14 Principles

1. Customer Obsession

Leaders start with the customer and work backwards. They work vigorously to earn and keep customer trust. Although leaders pay attention to competitors, they obsess over customers.

2. Ownership

Leaders are owners. They think long term and don't sacrifice long-term value for short-term results. They act on behalf of the entire company, beyond just their own team. They never say "that's not my job."

3. Invent and Simplify

Leaders expect and require innovation and invention from their teams and always find ways to simplify. They are externally aware, look for new ideas from everywhere, and are not limited by "not invented here." As we do new things, we accept that we may be misunderstood for long periods of time.

4. Are Right, A Lot

Leaders are right a lot. They have strong judgment and good instincts. They seek diverse perspectives and work to disconfirm their beliefs.

5. Learn and Be Curious

Leaders are never done learning and always seek to improve themselves. They are curious about new possibilities and act to explore them.

6. Hire and Develop the Best

Leaders raise the performance bar with every hire and promotion. They recognize exceptional talent, and willingly move them throughout the organization. Leaders develop leaders and take seriously their role in coaching others. We work on behalf of our people to invent mechanisms for development like Career Choice.

7. Insist on the Highest Standards

Leaders have relentlessly high standards — many people may think these standards are unreasonably high. Leaders are continually raising the bar and drive their teams to deliver high quality products, services, and processes. Leaders ensure that defects do not get sent down the line and that problems are fixed so they stay fixed.

8. Think Big

Thinking small is a self-fulfilling prophecy. Leaders create and communicate a bold direction that inspires results. They think differently and look around corners for ways to serve customers.

9. Bias for Action

Speed matters in business. Many decisions and actions are reversible and do not need extensive study. We value calculated risk taking.

10. Frugality

Accomplish more with less. Constraints breed resourcefulness, self-sufficiency, and invention. There are no extra points for growing headcount, budget size, or fixed expense.

11. Earn Trust

Leaders listen attentively, speak candidly, and treat others respectfully. They are vocally self-critical, even when doing so is awkward or embarrassing. Leaders do not believe their or their team's body odor smells of perfume. They benchmark themselves and their teams against the best.

12. Dive Deep

Leaders operate at all levels, stay connected to the details, audit frequently, and are skeptical when metrics and anecdote differ. No task is beneath them.

13. Have Backbone; Disagree and Commit

Leaders are obligated to respectfully challenge decisions when they disagree, even when doing so is uncomfortable or exhausting. Leaders have conviction and are tenacious. They do not compromise for the sake of social cohesion. Once a decision is determined, they commit wholly.

14. Deliver Results

Leaders focus on the key inputs for their business and deliver them with the right quality and in a timely fashion. Despite setbacks, they rise to the occasion and never settle.

Musashi and Bezos both believed in keeping a simple philosophical thread that would run through everything they did:

"If you know the way broadly, you will see it in everything."

-Miyamoto Musashi

"We've had three big ideas at Amazon that we've stuck with for 18 years, and they're the reason we're successful: Put the customer first. Invent. And be patient."

-Jeff Bezos

Incredible Self Belief and Growth Mindset: Conor McGregor and Kanye West

> *"From nothing, to something, to everything."*
> *-Conor McGregor*

Billionaire artist and entrepreneur Kanye West and record-breaking earner and former two-division UFC world champion Conor McGregor both came from humble beginnings, but were still able to achieve record-breaking financial success in their field, along with worldwide recognition of their accomplishments.

They have each openly talked about the power of self belief and mindset.

It is best illustrated in their words, and it is clear that an almost "delusional" self confidence played an obvious part in their tremendous achievements.

Incredible Self Belief

Kanye West:

"I always feel like I can do anything. That's the main thing people are controlled by: thoughts and perceptions of yourself. If you're taught you can't do anything, you won't do anything."

"People always tell you 'Be humble. Be humble.' When was the last time someone told you to be amazing? Be great! Be awesome!"

"Nobody can tell me where I can and can't go."

"You've got to be really dialled into exactly who you are to the one hundredth power or you're just like everyone else."

"Most people are slowed down by the perception of themselves. If you're taught you can't do anything, you won't do anything. I was taught I can do everything."

Conor McGregor:

"I always knew I only need one chance. I always felt like I was better than everybody. I always felt all I needed to do was get in there once. Give me one shot and I'll take it home."

"Many times I was laughed at and not believed in. Nothing external can defeat the internal. The only thing that can take someone down or break you down is internal. Nothing external is strong enough. It's just about making sure your internal dialogue and your internal belief in yourself is strong enough, that it can withstand the external. Understand, embrace, and accept the external, but don't let it seep in to your internal dialogue. It's a daily constant thing not to let the external infiltrate your internal."

"They love me because I love myself."

"Never give up on your dream. Be your own inspiration, a beacon of self-belief. Keep proving others wrong. If your dream doesn't scare you, it's not big enough."

Growth Mindset

Kanye West:

"I was never really good at anything except for the ability to learn."

"I'm not comfortable with comfort. I'm only comfortable when I'm in a place where I'm constantly learning and growing."

Conor McGregor:

"If they can do it, I can do it. I'm going to learn about it, study it."

"It's just about commitment, that's it. There is no secret sauce to this. Recognize what you need to do and do it, and you will succeed."

"You are an imitator. I am an innovator."

Both West and McGregor are groundbreaking pioneers who have achieved best-in-class success in their field. Their simple formula: Incredible self belief plus a continuous growth mindset...always looking to learn and improve.

Work Ethic and Daily Routine: Jocko Willink and Elon Musk

> *"Discipline equals freedom."*
> *-Jocko Willink*

Jocko Willink is a retired Navy SEAL commander.

According to his online bio:

"Jocko spent 20 years in the U.S. Navy SEAL Teams, starting as an enlisted SEAL and rising through the ranks to become a SEAL officer.

As commander of SEAL Team Three's Task Unit Bruiser during the battle of Ramadi, he orchestrated SEAL operations that helped the "Ready First" Brigade of the US Army's First Armored Division bring stability to the violent, war-torn city. Task Unit Bruiser became the most highly decorated Special Operations Unit of the Iraq War.

During his career, Jocko was awarded the Silver Star, the Bronze Star, and numerous other personal and unit awards. In 2010, Jocko retired from the Navy and launched Echelon Front where he teaches the leadership principles he learned on the battlefield to help others lead and win."

He is also the bestselling author of 10 books, including the classic peak performance and leadership books "Discipline Equals Freedom" and "Extreme Ownership".

In addition, he is a Brazilian Jiu Jitsu black belt, successful businessman, sought after leadership expert, and a top podcast host.

Jocko Willink gets a lot done.

Engineer and entrepreneur Elon Musk has founded three billion-dollar companies in PayPal, Tesla, and SpaceX.

Musk is known as more of "general" than a CEO. He believes he has to do what he does to save the human race. He has been referred to as "harsh", but does so because he believes the stakes are high.

He gets a lot done.

The secret of their success can be found in their work ethic and daily routine.

Work Ethic

Jocko Willink on the mindset of hard work:

"Hell week was not that hard to me. All I had to do was not quit."

"You already know what the right thing to do is. You just gotta do it."

"Life will try to stop you. Keep moving. Keep moving. KEEP MOVING."

Elon Musk on going "all in":

"I wish I could not eat so I could work more."

"What am I willing to sacrifice? Everything that other people hold dear."

"The harder it gets, the better I get."

"We're going to make it happen. As God is my bloody witness, I'm hell-bent on making it work."

"Persistence is very important. You should not give up unless you are forced to give up."

Daily Routine
Willink:

Wakes up every morning, including weekends, at 4:30 a.m.

He noticed early in his SEAL career that the best performers he served with woke up the earliest, starting their days while others were still in bed.

Does not eat breakfast.

Goes to his garage gym to work out for around an hour, not including cardio.

Goes to a San Diego beach following his workout for a short surfing session.

Showers and begins his to-do list. This can include: hours of research for his podcast, and/or working with his Echelon Front leadership clients over email, phone, or in-person. Echelon Front works with top-level businesses and organizations such as Fortune 500 companies and a Major League Baseball team.

Lunch between 11 and noon. He follows the Paleo-style diet, which is a low carbohydrate diet comprised of meats, fish, nuts, fruits, and vegetables.

Working on his product companies and writing a book fills out the afternoon.

End of the day Brazilian jiu-jitsu training at the San Diego gym he co-owns.

Paleo-style dinner at 8pm.

Family time.

Goes to sleep around 11:00 after planning and preparing for the next day.

Musk:

Wakes up at 7:00 a.m. after around six hours of sleep.

Showers but usually skips breakfast.

Sets in motion an intense schedule that breaks his time into five-minute time-blocked increments.

Works 85 to 100 hours a week, spending what he estimates to be 80% of his time on design and engineering.

He doesn't spend much time on meals during the day. He usually eats his lunch at a meeting. He eats most of his daily calories at business dinners.

Despite his busy schedule, he still carves out important time to read. He has a penchant for biographies of visionaries and innovators: Benjamin Franklin: An American Life and Einstein: His Life and Universe (both books written by the brilliant Walter Isaacson), and Howard Hughes: His Life and Madness' by Donald L. Barlett and James B. Steele.

Goes to bed around 1:00 a.m.

In conclusion, the daily routines and habits of Jocko Willink and Elon Musk are the absolute foundations of their success.

Deep Learning: Georges St. Pierre and Warren Buffett

> *"A great secret is that Warren and I are good at lifelong learning. If you keep learning all the time, you have a huge advantage."*
> -Charlie Munger, partner at Berkshire Hathaway

The Greatest Investor Of All Time

Billionaire Warren Buffett, one of the wealthiest men on the planet, has deeply committed to lifelong learning. He is ultra-focused on his business goals, and he has identified continuous learning as a key factor in achieving them. Nearly everything else in his work life is disregarded. Reading about and studying companies is the key fundamental that has driven Buffett's unparalleled investing success. He spends 5-6 hours a day reading on average 500 pages.

According to world renowned business and leadership expert Brian Tracy: "Warren Buffett reads 500 pages a day. He organizes his life so he works 2 to 3 hours, and reads the rest of the time. Warren said his secret to success is this: I just say no to everything that is not moving me toward my one or two most important goals."

He is committed to "saying no 99 times out of 100 to solicitation of his time or attention."

"Everyone can read what I read. It's a level playing field." says Buffett. Anyone can have access to and read the same things he does. But he is the one who takes the time to do it. He is very competitive, and sees reading as a fundamental advantage over his competition.

He sits in his office alone, and reads and reads the same things that anyone else can read. He loves the idea that he's going to win, because he's the one taking the time and making the sacrifices to get it done.

According to bestselling author and business expert Michael Simmons, "Warren Buffett spends 80 percent of his time reading and thinking, and has done so for his entire career."

Buffet also believes in learning from mentors. He was mentored by legendary economist, author, and Columbia University professor Benjamin Graham.

Additionally, Buffett keeps an open mind and subscribes to the philosophy of "not holding on to any strong beliefs when there could be proof you are wrong". He makes the effort to throw out one belief every year.

Buffet's key to success in his words:

"The difference between successful people and really successful people is that really successful people say no to almost everything. I just say no to everything that is not moving me toward my one or two most important goals."

The Greatest Mixed Martial Artist Of All Time

George's St. Pierre is a Canadian mma fighter and two-division UFC world champion. He is one of only seven fighters in history to ever achieve this accomplishment. He is regarded by many as the greatest mixed martial artist of all time. He believes deeply in continuous learning and improvement.

Just like Buffet, St. Pierre sees learning as a competitive edge. In his words:

"A guy that has more knowledge has the advantage."

On keeping a learning mindset:

"I keep the white-belt mentality that I can learn from anyone, anywhere, anytime."

On small continuous improvements:

"One of the lessons I learned in all those years practicing karate is that progress only comes in small incremental portions."

On why he seeks wisdom:

"Power is different when you combined it with wisdom. Wisdom allows you to use less power to accomplish more tasks."

St. Pierre has literally sought out and trained under some of the best coaches on the planet. Here's the list:

John Danaher, widely regarded as one of the best Brazilian Jiu Jitsu coaches on the planet

Firas Zahabi, widely regarded as one of the best mixed martial arts coaches on the planet

Greg Jackson, widely regarded as one of the best mixed martial arts coaches on the planet

Freddie Roach, widely regarded as one of the best boxing coaches on the planet

There may not be another martial artist alive who has trained with and learned from more of the best coaches in the world.

In conclusion: Both the greatest investor of all time and the greatest mixed martial artist of all time believe in deep learning and knowledge as an essential key competitive advantage. Success leaves clues.

Chapter Summary

1. Simplicity and Narrow Focus, Big Vision and Living Limitless: Bruce Lee and Steve Jobs
2. Simple Guiding Philosophy: Miyamoto Musashi and Jeff Bezos
3. Incredible Self Belief and Growth Mindset: Conor McGregor and Kanye West
4. Work Ethic and Daily Routine: Jocko Willink and Elon Musk
5. Deep Learning: Georges St. Pierre and Warren Buffett

Key Lessons:

1. Simplify.
2. Keep your focus narrow.
3. Have a big vision and live limitless.
4. Create a simple guiding philosophy for your business and life, and stick to it.
5. Do everything you can to develop incredible self belief.
6. Keep a growth mindset.
7. Work ethic and daily routine are the absolute foundations of success.
8. Knowledge acquired through deep learning is an essential key competitive advantage.

15 Lessons For A New Martial Artist And Leader

> *"Magic is just someone spending more time on something than anyone else might reasonably expect."*
> *-Raymond Joseph Teller(Penn and Teller)*

Looking back on the last 15 years of training, I have been blessed and fortunate to do something I love with great people who made me not just a better martial artist, but also a better person.

Each martial arts lesson has an accompanying leadership application.

Here are the 15 thoughts I would share with my beginner self 15 years ago:

1. Show up.

Martial arts: 90% of success is showing up. Stop thinking. Just do it.

Leadership: A true test of a leader is showing up and energizing your team on the days you don't feel like it. You may be stressed, tired, or sick, but you still have to be able to rise to the occasion and energize.

2. Be brilliant at the basics.

Martial arts: Don't get bored with the basics. Have fun with the fundamentals. The simple foundational techniques you learn in your first year of training will make up 90% of what you'll use for the next 15 years.

Leadership: Forget the fancy stuff and the latest "flavor of the week" management techniques. Focus on the simple fundamentals like leading by example, being a deep learner, expert listening, upholding standards, and energizing others.

3. Invest in yourself.

Martial arts: The best investment you'll ever make is in YOURSELF. Find the best coaches you CANNOT afford. Sacrifice the little unnecessary expenditures so you can invest in yourself. I was fortunate to have outstanding coaches who prioritized fundamentals, conditioning, respect, and honor.

Leadership: Invest in self education and improvement. One way to do this is to find the best coaches and advisors you can in the most important areas of your life: fitness, nutrition, health, leadership, finances, business, relationships, and happiness. Have the highest standards for yourself and who you surround yourself with.

4. Slow down.

Martial arts: Slow down to speed up success. Take your time and practice slowly to "groove in" solid technique. Your success is a marathon, not a sprint.

Leadership: Focus on the long game. Haste makes waste. You can operate with a sense of urgency, and at same avoid being reckless.

Slow is smooth. Smooth is fast. Billionaires Jeff Bezos and Warren Buffett both had the patience to focus on a longer game, and it paid off.

5. Do more of what you love and less of what you don't.

Martial arts: If you don't love the training, your coaches, and your teammates, find somewhere that you do.

Leadership: If you are not having fun the majority of the time as a leader, you're not going to be effective. You will not be able to compete over the long term with leaders and organizations who are having fun and are energized by what they do. Loving the work you do and the people you do it with gives you the energy to succeed at the highest level. If you're not having fun, find somewhere that you do.

6. Safety is most important.

Martial arts: If you're injured, you can't train. If you can't train, you can't get better. Be a safe training partner. Be your brother's and sister's keeper. There are thousands of ways to injure yourself in mixed martial arts training. Find partners and coaches who can PUSH you, but not recklessly injure you.

Leadership: Creating a safe environment for members of your organization is crucial to attracting and keeping great people. A toxic work environment creates tremendous stress on people. It can have a negative effect their health. It can have a negative effect on their relationships and happiness outside of work. You must continuously listen to the challenges your people are facing on a day-to-day basis. This can be done in one-on-one conversations, meetings that are solely meant for leadership listening, and anonymous satisfaction surveys. Additionally, do everything you can to eliminate mindless negativity of gossiping, complaining, condemning, blaming, and venting. This type of communication creates a tremendous drain on everyone.

7. Stand next to the best person in the room.

Martial arts: Surround yourself with people smarter, stronger, and better than you. Positive peer pressure is one of the most powerful forces in the universe.

Leadership: Surround yourself with the best and brightest people you can. And don't demotivate them. Surround yourself with those who have strengths in the areas you don't, so you can focus on what you do best and share your unique, special gifts with the world.

8. Focus on the few, not the many.

Martial arts: You don't need 10,000 techniques to be good. "I fear not the man who has practiced 10,000 kicks once, but I fear the man who has practiced one kick 10,000 times. -Bruce Lee"

Leadership: Keep your focus as narrow as possible. Work in the areas of your one or two greatest strengths, and delegate or say no to everything else. Focus on the one or two vital functions that really move the needle in your organization.

9. Be a lifter, not a leaner.

Martial arts: Bring good energy to the training. Leave your problems at the door, and LOCK IN.

Leadership: As a leader, it is your job to bring the energy of certainty, enthusiasm, and expert listening. The opposite of this is doubt, indifference, and distractedness in conversations and meetings. Lead by example and bring the right kind of energy each day.

10. Give your best effort...what ever it is that day.

Martial arts: Each day, your best effort will be different. What matters, is that you give that day's best.

Leadership: As P90x creator Tony Horton says, "do your best and forget the rest". As long as you are:

1. Doing your best each day,
2. Not hurting anyone,
3. Doing things legally, morally and ethically, and
4. Trying to go to bed a little smarter and a little better than when you woke up,

You should have confidence in yourself and know that you are on the right path.

11. Take care of your machine.

Martial arts: When you're 20, treat your body like it's 40, and you'll have a long and healthy training life.

Leadership: If you are not regularly taking care of your health and good brain chemistry through quality sleep, regular exercise, and good nutrition, you will always be performing at a deficit and leaving something on the table as a leader.

12. Look for the elite edge.

Martial arts: Get under the bar. Lift some weights. Technique is most important, but strength + technique is unquestionably a level up.

Leadership: Expertise is the greatest competitive advantage. Spend time every day on self education. This can come in the form of books, podcasts, coaches, mentors, etc.

13. Keep a white belt mentality.

Martial arts: You can't learn with your mouth open. Listen to your coaches. Never stop listening and learning.

Leadership: Wake up everyday with curiosity. Throw out ideas and beliefs that are no longer serving you. Never ever think that you know everything. Never underestimate how wrong you can be. Keep your mind open.

14. Be a "success celebrator".

Martial arts: Celebrate the success and accomplishments of your teammates. Nobody wants to be around an energy vampire.

Leadership: Catch people doing things right every day. Too many leaders only catch people doing things wrong. Celebrate small wins with the team. Praise in public, and keep criticisms private.

15. Be grateful.

Martial arts: There are many people out there who wish they had the opportunity to train, but for reasons outside of their control, they cannot. Be grateful for your training partners, coaches, and for the simple physical ability to walk onto the mat each day.

Leadership: Leadership is a privilege and an honor, not a right or a burden. Not every day will be rainbows and roses, but be grateful you're in a position to have a positive effect on others.

That is all.

Now go train and lead.

SELF PROTECTION PILLAR ONE: AWARENESS AND AVOIDANCE

> *"Self protection encompasses everything from internet safety, to how I drive. I drive in a defensive manner with two hands on the wheel, because my mindset is "anything can happen at any moment". The self protection mindset is constantly being prepared for something to happen. Even what I eat and drink is self protection, because it is preparing me and keeping me healthy."*
>
> *-Paul Sharp*

Our Three Pillars of Self Protection are:

1. Awareness and Avoidance
2. Attitude
3. Animal

Each of the Three Pillars will be covered in depth through principles. Each principle will have a self protection application, as well as a leadership application.

We'll begin with our first pillar: Awareness and Avoidance.

It is by far the most important pillar of the three. If you only remember one thing from this book it is this: be aware of where serious problems happen, and avoid those places at all cost.

Don't overthink this.

It's not that complicated.

PRINCIPLE #1:

Be Your Own Protector

> *"The true secret is to never be dependent on anything. Once you're dependent, you will always have insecurity."*
> —Firas Zahabi

Self protection application

When facing a situation where you must defend your life, you must have the mentality that no one is coming to save you. You must be your own personal security team.

Rely on nothing and rely on no one.

Do not expect the police to get there in time if someone is trying to hurt you, or even worse abduct you or take your life.

You must take 100% responsibility for your own safety.

World-renowned self protection expert Tony Blauer says: "Be your own bodyguard".

Retired Army Delta Force operator Pat McNamara says: "Be the agent in charge of your executive protection detail".

Be your own best friend and your own protector.

> "One of the greatest things you can do in your life is become your own best friend."
> -Joseph Rodrigues

Leadership application

No one is coming to turn you into a better leader. Take 100% responsibility for becoming the best leader you can be. Self educate. Read and study great leadership. Seek out coaches and mentors who you can not only learn from, but who will tell you your blind spots and where you can improve.

PRINCIPLE #2:

Don't Be There

> *"It is remarkable how much long-term advantage people like us have gotten by trying to be consistently not stupid, instead of trying to be very intelligent."*
> —Charlie Munger, billionaire partner at Berkshire Hathaway

Self protection application

99.9% of self protection is the awareness and avoidance of violence. Ask yourself, "What advice would I give to someone I care about that would keep them safe?" Take that same advice for yourself. Life a safe lifestyle. You already know how to do this. A safe lifestyle:

Lock your doors

Avoid being alone in bad places

Don't drive aggressively

Etc.

You already know how to do this.

Always trust your gut. It is never wrong. If something feels wrong about a person or situation, avoid it and get away as fast as you can. Military special forces operators always look for the tactical advantage. One tactical advantage is avoiding unnecessary damage and risk.

When planning the strategy for his fighter, Greg Jackson (coach and head trainer of MMA/UFC champions Jon Jones, Georges St. Pierre, and Holly Holm) first looks to "avoid the specific points that can lead to everything bad that can happen to you". This is avoidance. Avoiding the opponent's strengths.

Chris Sutton, founder of "C.O.B.R.A Self Defense", has a simple and brilliant saying: "Don't let the bad guy control the time and place."

Follow the "10pm Rule". Nothing good happens after 10pm, so you might as well be at home and much safer.

> "One of the greatest ways to avoid trouble is to keep it simple."
> -Charlie Munger

Leadership application
99.9% of success is in the setup.

A big component of successful setup as a leader is avoidance:

Avoid hiring the wrong people.

Avoid promoting the wrong person into a leadership position.

Avoid the wrong business partnership.

Avoid working for the wrong person or company.

Avoid focusing on the wrong things in the business.

Avoid starting the wrong business.

Avoid bad business investments.

How do you avoid bad situations?

1. Have clear and simple principles and criteria for every decision you make. Example criteria for someone you would look to hire: High Energy, High Standards, High Warmth. Example criteria for starting up (or investing in) a business: a competitive advantage, an experienced and passionate operator, solves an underserved problem or need, and a clear and simple plan.

2. Investigate, investigate investigate. Then investigate some more. Look for red flags and reasons FIRST to not to do the deal, to not to hire or promote someone, or to not get involved in a partnership. If the red flags are exhausted first and your "downside is protected" now the upside can begin to take care of itself.

3. Always trust your gut. It is never wrong. If something feels wrong about a person or situation, avoid it and get away as fast as you can.

Minimize your risk and downside.

An ounce of prevention is worth a pound of cure.

PRINCIPLE #3:

Sheepdog Mentality

> *"Competence, caring, and conviction combine to form a fundamental element shaping the fighting spirit of your troops."*
> -Jim Mattis, ret. General U.S. Marines

Self-protection application

Pat McNamara, retired Delta Force operator, on staying sheepdog:

"You are the agent in charge of your own executive protection detail. Your loved ones are counting on you. Remember why you are staying fit, staying smart, and keeping your skills up. Stay sheepdog."

The Sheepdog mentality as articulated by U.S. Army veteran Eric Milzarski in his article on the "WeAreTheMighty" website:

"The analogy is simple. There are three types of people in this world: sheep, wolves, and sheepdogs. The vast majority of people are sheep — nothing wrong with that. They move about their day carelessly, are loving and compassionate beasts, and only rarely, accidentally hurt each other. The wolves want to devour the sheep. They'll cause as much harm as they can with little remorse. These are the terrorists, despots, dictators, and other types of villains in this world.

Which brings us to the sheepdog, the guardian of the sheep against the wolves. Their capacity for violence is frowned on by the sheep. Their capacity for love is frowned on by the wolves. The sheepdog is bound by duty in that middle ground. They are the troops, first-responders, and anyone willing to take a stand against the evils of this world.

The goal of the sheepdog is to prevent violence and keep the blissful sheep safe. The sheepdog isn't actively seeking to harm others— that's the work of a wolf. The sheepdog is defined not by his hatred of wolves, desire for violence, or any similarity that blur the line between wolf and sheepdog. They are not defined by the reasons why they're not sheep.

It's the love and compassion for those who cannot defend themselves that truly defines a sheepdog. It's what makes us different from the wolves."

> *"Safety is the single most important piece of foundation needed for great culture."*
> -Daniel Coyle, The Culture Code

Leadership application

Put the success and happiness of your team before your own.

Make those who follow you feel safe.

Practiced heart-centered listening. Let them know that their opinions and feelings are respected and valued. Let them them know that they will not be punished for having opinions that are different than yours.

Protect your team members from mistreatment from co-workers, managers, and those outside of your organization.

Have the courage to stand up for your people.

SELF PROTECTION
PILLAR TWO: ATTITUDE

> *"As a young hustler, 50 Cent quickly learned the value of boldness, how he could push others on their heels by feeling supreme confidence in himself."*
> -Robert Greene

Practicing a confident, assertive attitude on a daily basis is one of the greatest ways to deter an attack. Be that attack mental, emotional, or physical.

You must project an attitude of confidence outward to the world. Mental, emotional, and physical confidence.

Working to improve your confidence is easily one of the best things you can ever do for yourself.

We'll cover exactly how to sharpen your attitude and confidence in the following chapters. If you're not already practicing some of the things we'll discuss, they can be life changing when you begin to apply them.

PRINCIPLE #4:

Attitude Is A Weapon

> *"Marines believe that attitude is a weapon system."*
> -General Jim Mattis

Self protection application

People with confident attitudes make hard targets. If you carry yourself with mental, emotional, and physical confidence in your everyday life, you will find for the most part that people will simply leave you alone.

Confidence is something that can be practiced and developed.

1) Stand up straight and look people in the eye.
2) Don't put up with mistreatment.
3) Build your body up to be physically strong and capable. This doesn't mean you have to spend 20 hours a week in the gym. It means simply being in the best shape you can be in the time that you have. Lift heavy things once or twice a week. Sprint once or twice a week. Hire a reputable, experienced trainer to help you (this can be a tremendous investment in yourself).
4) Learn to defend yourself. Take Brazilian Jiu Jitsu classes, boxing classes, mma training, etc.

5) Surround yourself with confident people who celebrate your success.

6) Work on your "self talk". A great book on the subject is "What To Say When You Talk To Yourself" by Dr. Shad Helmstetter

7) Get good at something. Figure out what your one or two natural strengths are, and spend an hour a day working on improving them. This will lead to you becoming an expert at something. Being an expert at something gives you tremendous confidence.

We have the potential to be attacked far more on a daily basis emotionally than we have the potential to be attacked physically.

By standing up for yourself daily and also working on your confidence, you will turn your attitude into a weapon. This leads to reducing the chances you will ever be attacked physically.

Predators want an soft, easy target. Someone with a confident physical and mental attitude is the opposite. They are a hard target.

> *"Your confidence level determines your life."*
> *-Dre Baldwin*

Leadership application

Leadership Confidence = Certainty and Enthusiasm

As a leader, your attitude of "Certainty and Enthusiasm" is a weapon against mediocrity and unhappiness in your team and in your organization.

You must "bring the juice" every day. The juice is that energy of Certainty and Enthusiasm that is contagious to everyone around you.

Additionally, you must go into every situation with the attitude of: I am respectful, but not fearful.

Confidence is contagious. So is doubt (much more so than confidence).

PRINCIPLE #5:

Never See Yourself On The Losing Side Of Violence

> *"I often tell my clients that visualization is like bringing a gun to a knife fight: your previously negative thoughts and self-talk won't stand a chance against the more powerful detailed visions of success you are about to create."*
>
> *-Dr. Jason Selk*

Self protection application

When you are thinking about what a violent encounter where you must defend your life or someone else's, never imagine yourself on the losing end. This is bad programming. You are programming yourself to fail.

The mind can't tell the difference between "mental rehearsal" and the real life thing.

Use your imagination to see yourself fighting off the attacker and going home safely to your family. Imagine yourself overcoming adversity. This is the only "movie" that you want to watch in your head when it comes to violence.

> *"Physical dominance can make you great. Mental dominance is what ultimately will make you unstoppable."*
>
> *-Tim Grover, author of "Relentless"*

Leadership application

Be the "chief visionary" to your team and organization. As the late Steve Jobs said, you must "project the future".

Never see your team members or organization failing. Instead, see a positive vision of the future in your mind. Visualize your past triumphs. See yourself, your team, and your organization as the best version it can be. Imagine yourself, your team, and your organization achieving your dream goal.

Over-communicate that positive vision over and over again to all your team members. Never show doubt in the vision.

PRINCIPLE #6:

Mental, Emotional, and Physical Posture

> *"Get your act together. Stand up straight with your shoulders back. It's a powerful position because it means you're brave enough to take what's coming."*
>
> -Dr. Jordan Peterson

Self protection application

Strong posture = hard target.

Poor posture = easy target.

One of the easiest ways to avoid violence is not to look, act, think, and talk like a victim. To think and do *the opposite* of what a victim thinks and does.

Strong "physical posture" is standing up straight and looking people in the eye. It is being physically fit. It is strengthening your posterior muscles, and stretching and opening your anterior muscles so you "stand up straighter". It is also walking and moving with confidence and purpose.

Strong "mental posture" is seeing yourself as a capable person who is worthy of love. It is living the life you want to live without letting anyone change your mind about any of that. It is knowing that you put the repetitions in to become great at what you do.

Strong "emotional posture" is standing up for yourself on a regular basis. It is not putting up with mistreatment. It is not quitting when things get tough.

> "Research shows that attitudes follow behavior – if we act in a certain way, over time our attitudes follow. The emotions you express, such as confidence or happiness, are contagious –they influence those around you."
> -Jeffrey Pfeffer

Leadership application

People want to follow those who have a strong physical, mental, and emotional posture. Strong posture is equated to confidence. Confidence is equated to good leadership.

Strong posture and leadership confidence comes from putting in the repetitions to achieve expertise. It comes from positive self talk and positive visualization.

It comes from doing the right things. Legally, equitably, ethically. It comes from giving your best effort every day, especially when you don't feel like it. Work to develop your strong posture and leadership confidence every day.

PRINCIPLE #7:

The Power Of No

> *"No" is a word that must never be negotiated, because the person who chooses not to hear it is trying to control you...Declining to hear "no" is a signal that someone is either seeking control or refusing to relinquish it."*
>
> -Gavin de Becker

Self protection application

"No" is a complete sentence.

You can exercise your "no muscle" every day.

Say no to mistreatment.

Say no to those who waste your time and drain your energy.

Say no to those who don't want the best for you.

Say NO to someone who wants to hurt you or people you care about.

By exercising your "no muscle" every day, you will be far more capable of bringing out your "Power of No" when you need it the most.

Your voice is a powerful weapon. In a situation where someone is trying to bring you physical harm, you must be able to say "NO" so loud and clear so that person feels your righteous anger and defiance from every single cell of your body.

> *"When we say no, after the initial, short-term annoyance, disappointment, or anger of the other person wears off, the respect kicks in. When we push back effectively, it shows people that your time is highly valuable. It distinguishes the professional from the amateur."*
> —Greg McKeown

Leadership application

Saying "yes" is a tremendous time waster.

We must learn to say no to the things that don't get us closer to our most important goals.

We must learn to say no to spending time with people who do not bring us joy or growth.

We must say no to the negative thoughts and limiting beliefs that hold us back.

We must say no to the distractions that do not allow us to best share our special gifts, thus benefiting the world around us.

PRINCIPLE #8:

Capable Of Cruelty

> *"Stand up for yourself like a respectable human being and be a little bit of a light on the world instead of a blight."*
> —Dr. Jordan Peterson

Self protection application

We must take the following mental, physical, and emotional posture:

"I am kind and respectful, but do not cross me. Because if you cross me and mistreat me, I will make it very uncomfortable for you."

We must be capable of cruelty. That does not mean that we use this cruelty every day. We only need to use it if we are under attack mentally, emotionally, or physically.

Being capable of cruelty is:

1. Firmly standing up for yourself if you are being bullied or mistreated.
2. Ferociously fighting back with every single ounce of your being if you are being attacked physically.

Most of the time, simply being capable of cruelty is enough to prevent any attacks on us to happen in the first place. Bullies and criminals want easy targets. People who are capable of cruelty and ferociously fighting back are not easy targets.

> *"It's not what you preach. It's what you tolerate."*
> *-Jocko Willink, ret Navy SEAL commander*

Leadership application

As a leader, you must be able to challenge people directly, and never walk by mediocrity without addressing it. For our leadership purposes, we will define "cruelty" as the following:

Tough love, straightforward honesty, constructive feedback, directness without removing the dignity of the receiver.

Advice from two-time Super Bowl champion coach Bill Parcells

"You have to be honest with people — brutally honest. You have to tell them the truth about their performance, you have to tell it to them face-to-face, and you have to tell it to them over and over again.

Sometimes the truth will be painful, and sometimes saying it will lead to an uncomfortable confrontation.

So be it. The only way to change people is to tell them in the clearest possible terms what they're doing wrong.

And if they don't want to listen, they don't belong on the team."

The following story by Todd Herman, peak performance expert coach and bestselling author of "Alter Ego", illustrates a similar point to Parcells:

"A study brought two businessmen that looked and were dressed the same into a restaurant.

One businessman was curt to the point of being rude, but not quite rude, and complained about all the things that weren't right and where the quality wasn't there to the waitress.

The other was kind, joked around with the waitress, and was overtly kind.

They then asked all the diners in the restaurant which one of the two men did they like.

They chose the kind man.

Then they asked the diners which man that they thought was more successful in life.

The majority chose the man who was curt and short.

Then they asked which one of the two men would you rather work for. Almost everyone said the man who was curt.

They asked them why. Because he knows what he wants, and you know where you stand with someone like that.

A lot of the platitudes that have been passed around in self help and personal development books are not based in true human psychology.

People talk in business that before someone buys from you, they have to know, like, and trust you.

I believe they have to know you, respect you, and trust you."

As leaders, we must be capable of having difficult conversations. When you truly care about the success and happiness of your team members, they will allow you to have the difficult, straightforward conversations.

PRINCIPLE #9:

Do The Single Hardest Thing (Get Comfortable With Discomfort)

> *"Making yourself uncomfortable speeds up the process of mental toughness."*
>
> -Dr. Jason Selk

Self protection application

Do something that makes you uncomfortable every day.

By doing this, you are mentally, physically, and emotionally preparing yourself for if you ever have to defend your life against an attacker

Ask yourself this in any situation:

What's the single hardest thing I can do?

Do that.

It might be having a difficult conversation with someone.

It might be taking the stairs instead of the elevator.

It might be eating the chicken breast instead of the cheeseburger.

Single = the one thing

Hardest = emotionally most difficult

Author of "Facing Violence" and highly respected self-defense expert and instructor Rory Miller on "eating frogs":

"You won't enjoy defending yourself from an assault.

Make it a habit to do the things you don't enjoy.

Immediately, efficiently and without hesitation. If you are going to jump in the cold water, jump.

Don't work yourself up to it. As long as it is safe (the water is deep enough, no rocks…) jump. Jump with your whole heart.

If the very idea of competing in a tournament makes you nervous, you must do it. That is fear, a low level fear, and facing fear is the essence of self-defense.

Everyone should experience rough impact. Microconcussions are bad, and I don't recommend people box for long, but everyone who is interested not just in self-defense but in who they really are, should experience boxing.

Taking a hit, keeping cool or finding useful emotional triggers (either can work, both have limitations) and staying in the fight are invaluable skills.

So what is this drill, Frog Eating?

It is a habit. From this moment forward if there is something that needs to be done, you do it.

Decisively and immediately.

Constantly feel for your own glitches: the things that you fear or hate or that disgust you. If something is unpleasant, at any level, do that first.

Kill it. Without hesitation. But, like most of the life skills presented here, there is no downside.

What will your boss think of someone who does the hard stuff first and without complaining?

Will your family appreciate a you who gets stuff done?

Will you be setting an example to be proud of? Not only does this drill make you tougher, it also makes you smarter, and in the end, wiser.

The person who acts when everyone else hesitates is a hero. Eating Frogs becomes a super-power."

> *"If you are ever at the crossroads of making a difficult decision, always ask yourself, "What is the hard choice?". Then take that path."*
>
> *-Jerzy Gregorek*

Leadership application

Your success and happiness in life and leadership will be determined by the number of difficult things you do in a week.

The number of difficult conversations you have.

The extra time you spend reading and educating yourself instead of going out with friends on the weekend.

The going to the gym five days a week to keep your energy up so you can energize others.

The admitting when you made a mistake.

Make the hard choice every day. Your people will see this and respect you more for it.

PRINCIPLE #10:

Let People Keep Their Dignity (Verbal De-escalation And Diffusion)

> *"Most people don't want to fight that badly."*
> -John Danaher

Self protection application

In a social violence situation, most people want you to talk them out of the fight. If you can show them respect and let them keep their pride and dignity, most people will walk away without trying to fight you.

One of my favorite techniques when someone is hurling insults my way is simply to listen and say, "Okay". I am not disagreeing with them, and I am not "returning fire" with my own insults and escalating the situation. I am simply saying, "okay".

Your best mental, emotional, and physical posture when being confronted is this: I am respectful, but not fearful.

1. If you are not respectful, and not fearful, you may force an unnecessary fight to happen by showing disrespect. This is very bad. Fights can have legal or life changing consequences, or result in death.

2. If you are respectful, but fearful, you may become an easier target and an unnecessary victim because the aggressor saw the fear in you.
3. If you are not respectful and fearful, you will simply make everything worse.
4. Be respectful, but not fearful. This is the best mental, emotional, and physical posture you can have to deescalate a potentially violent situation and also avoid becoming a target in the first place.

Tim Larkin, self-defense expert instructor and author of "When Violence Is The Answer", covers the two types of violence on the "Art of Manliness" blog:

"It is essential we understand this distinction between social aggression and asocial violence right now.

Social aggression is about competition; asocial violence is about destruction.

Competition has rules; destruction has none.

Social aggression is about communication — implicitly with status indicators but explicitly with lots of taunting and posturing.

There is no talking with asocial violence.

Open your mouth and you are likely to eat a lightning-fast punch or a jacketed bullet traveling at 2,500 feet per second."

In most social violence situations, your attacker can be persuaded not to fight through deescalation techniques:

Listening

Agreeing

Apologizing

Keeping a safe space between you

Avoiding anything provocative

Keeping your words short and to the point

Letting them keep their dignity

As you are trying to deescalate the situation, you must also always be aware of your physical safety.

This means keeping a safe distance between you. Keeping your hands up in a "prayer" position at around your chest level in case you have to defend a physical attack. Paying attention to pre-assault cues such as them balling their fist up before they try to punch you. Always pay attention to what their hands are doing.

Never ever underestimate someone, no matter how physically small they are. They may have a weapon on them, or they may be a highly trained fighter.

Never hesitate to call 911, or have someone with you or in the crowd call. Many times, it's best to have the police deescalate the situation.

> *"Converse, don't confront."*
> *-Jim Ross*

Leadership application

You will have to have many difficult conversations as a leader. It may be with a team member, your boss, a co-worker, a business partner, etc.

When having frank conversations, it is absolutely possible to have discourse without disrespect.

Conversation without confrontation. To do this, you must first do everything you can to remove your emotions from the situation.

I prefer any difficult conversation to be done one-on-one whenever possible. It allows both parties to speak more freely and keep their dignity.

There are exceptions to this. Sometimes you need a witness for legal purposes, or someone else in the room for safety purposes.

I'll often visualize a difficult conversation in my imagination before I have it. This mental rehearsal is very useful. I will visualize it going well, and I'll also visualize the worst case scenarios that could happen. By imaging the worst, you are far more prepared to handle it when it happens.

Another tip: Praise in public, criticize in private.

When challenging team members to be better, it is best done privately, thus allowing them to keep their dignity.

Here are three tools for difficult conversations.

The Hard Truth Test

1. Is it true?
2. Does it benefit the person to hear it?
3. Is it emotionally difficult for you to have the conversation?

If it is 1) true 2) it benefits the person in the long run to hear it, and 3) it is emotionally difficult for you, then have the conversation.

Conversation (Not Confrontation) Framework

1. Make sure that it's true.
2. Ask them why it is happening.
3. Ask them how they will improve it in the future.
4. 100% believe in them that they can improve.
5. Always let them keep their dignity.
6. After the conversation, ask yourself, "What could I have done better as a leader to prevent this situation?", and "What can I do better as a leader in the future?"

Preparation Tips

A. Focus on the number one thing that they can improve (don't overload them).
B. Write out what you'll say. Make it brief and bright (short and positive). Short = not unnecessarily long. Positive = make it win-win conversation.
C. Practice. Before you have the conversation, say what you wrote out loud three times.
D. Visualize. Imagine the worst case scenario that could happen during the conversation. Make peace with it.
E. Practice one more time. Consider role playing the conversation out with someone you respect and trust, having that person play the role of the person you'll be talking to. When you're done, ask them for feedback.
F. Have the conversation. Regardless of the short term pain for either of you (or both of you). A little discomfort can lead to a lot growth.

PRINCIPLE #11:

Always Trust Your Gut

> *"We must learn and then teach our children that niceness does not equal goodness. Niceness is a decision, a strategy of social interaction; it is not a character trait. People seeking to control others almost always present the image of a nice person in the beginning."*
>
> -Gavin de Becker

Self protection application

If something feels wrong about a person or situation, get out of there without hesitation.

We all have an incredible sense of intuition that we are born with. Unfortunately, we do not always choose to listen to it. That internal protector is always switched on, ready to sound the alarm on dangerous situations. It is one of the most important and underrated aspects of self protection. Always trust your gut and always trust your feelings.

> *"Pay attention to whom your energy increases and decreases around, because that's the universe giving you a hint of who you should embrace or stray from."*
>
> -Wesley Snipes

Leadership application

Train yourself every day to listen to your intuition, no matter how softly it may speak. It is constantly giving you feedback. Always trust that gut intuition. It is never wrong.

As discussed in a previous chapter, if something feels wrong about a person or situation, avoid it and get away as quickly and decisively as you can.

Trust your gut to avoid hiring the wrong people.

Trust your gut to avoid promoting the wrong person into a leadership position.

Trust your gut to avoid the wrong business partnership.

Trust your gut to avoid working for the wrong person or company.

Trusting your gut is one of the most underrated success tools in business and leadership. Ignore it at your own peril.

SELF PROTECTION PILLAR THREE: ANIMAL

> *"I prefer to be a dead lion than a live dog. Never again bend my head, to take my eyes down, when I see somebody who thinks he is better than me. Nobody is better than me, and I am not better than anybody."*
> -Eitan Cohen, Senior counter terror and Krav Maga instructor, Israel military

Our third pillar of self protection is "Animal".

It is the ability to bring out the Animal you have inside in a situation where you have to defend your life or the life of another.

It is bringing out that inner animal for one simple purpose. It is a concept I personally learned from Richard Dimitri, one of the most respected and knowledgeable self protection experts on the planet:

"It's not about moves. It's about wanting to be able to go home and hug the people you care about most again. Find someone in your life that you can't live without, and imagine how they would feel if you wouldn't fight back for your life. The self defense objective: go back home and hug your loved ones."

If you are ever in the position where you have to defend your life against a physical attack, you must "go Animal".

This is how much smaller, untrained individuals defend themselves during home invasions, abduction attempts, and other horrific attacks perpetrated by bigger, stronger asocial predators.

Only 1% of what they do to fight back and get away to safety is due to technique. 99% of the reason they survive is due to their animal attitude and aggression unleashed on their attacker.

> *"In a self defense situation, you have a better chance to go berserk on your instincts than to try to pull some fancy moves. It happens too fast. Aim big and hit big. Keep it simple. It's gotta be simple and fast."*
> —Nick Drossos

Those who survive violent attacks are able to bring out the "Black Dog" inside of them that all of us have.

1. They fight back with maximum intensity.
2. They attack with animal attitude.
3. They use ruthless aggression to defeat superior size and strength.
4. They are fast, furious, and ferocious.

They become the "30 pound mountain lion that hasn't been fed in a week".

PRINCIPLE #12:

Fitness Is A Weapon (Stronger People Are Harder To Kill)

> *"As a police officer in Miami, at least once in your career, your physical fitness will determine whether you live or die."*
> —Tony Sentmanat, retired SWAT team officer

Self protection application

Defending you life against an attacker is an athletic endeavor.

It requires speed, strength and stamina, just like any other sport. You don't have to work on this for 15 hours a week like a professional athlete or bodybuilder. You simply want to be in YOUR best shape in the limited amount of time that you have to train.

Done the right way, this can be accomplished in as little as a few hours a week of focused, high-caliber training. Think about it as a marathon, not a sprint. Something you'll do consistently for years. Think consistency over intensity.

You want the right combination of strength and stamina/conditioning. An example of a good combination and schedule:

Monday: Conditioning

Tuesday: Total Body Strength

Wednesday: Recovery

Thursday: Conditioning

Friday: Total Body Strength

Saturday: Recovery

Sunday: Off

These sessions can be as short as 15-30 minutes each if they are focused and programmed properly for you by an experienced professional trainer you understands that your goals are tactical strength and conditioning.

If you are training for self protection, HIIT (High Intensity Interval Training) for conditioning and tactical strength training are a solid combination.

> "I found out within my first year as police officer, that just like being good at any athletic endeavor like football or baseball, you have to put the time into getting good at combatives."
> -Chad Lyman

The definition of tactical strength and conditioning by Drew Hammond from the Science For Sport website:

"Tactical strength and conditioning can be thought of as a multidisciplinary approach to the repair, maintenance, and performance optimisation of the tactical athlete in order to maximise their effectiveness on the battlefield. Bear in mind that the term "tactical athlete" could just as easily refer to police officers, Tier 1 soldiers, firefighters, or even emergency medical service personnel."

Self protection situations are almost always fast and furious, so training your conditioning at high intensity is useful. Some of my favorite high intensity conditioning moves are incline/hill sprints, burpees, sled pushes and drags, punching sprints on a heavy bag, and the rowing machine.

Some of my favorite tactical strength movements include sled pushes and pulls, farmers carries (and all types of weighted carries), rotational/transverse core work, trap bar deadlifts, dumbbell cleans dumbbell, overhead presses, dumbbell snatches, goblet or front squats, Turkish get-ups, pull-up variations, inverted rows on a TRX apparatus, medicine ball throws, sledgehammer slams, tire flips, and push-ups.

Recovery work can include stretching, foam rolling, mobility work, walking, etc.

An investment in a reputable personal trainer who has the knowledge and ability to train you like a tactical athlete is worth it's weight in gold.

I'm also a big proponent of the type metabolic circuit training offered at the F45 fitness centers around the world. Metabolic circuits are easily one of the most efficient and effective way to train.

> *"We all could be tactical athletes. Your fitness can be the difference between living or dying or saving a friend."*
> —Stew Smith, ret. Navy SEAL

Five outstanding books on strength and conditioning:

The New Rules Of Lifting by Alwyn Cosgrove

Maximum Strength by Eric Cressey

5/3/1 by Jim Wendler

100 Strength Training Tips For Combat Athletes by Brooks Kubik

Outstanding science-based strength and conditioning YouTube channels:

The Bioneer

AthleanX

Jeff Nippard

Jeremy Ethier

Bob and Brad (Physical Therapists)

Always talk to your doctor before starting a new workout program.

> *"No one who is operating at an elite level long-term is ignoring their health—in business or life. Physical fitness is not just about being ripped or strong; it is about having the energy needed to lead."*
> —Jason Redman, ret. Navy SEAL

Leadership application

Maximize your energy in order to energize others. The ability to energize others is absolutely crucial to your effectiveness as a leader.

Doing the right kind of physical exercise on a regular basis is a key component to maximizing your energy.

The right kind of exercise:

1. You feel energized when you're done with the workout
2. Your risk of injury is low
3. You enjoy the type of training you're doing
4. You enjoy the people you are doing it with

The right kind of exercise can be done in as little as fifteen to thirty minutes per day, five days per week.

Peak performance expert and bestselling author of "How To Fail At Everything And Still Win Big" Scott Adams of the auditing your energy:

"I recommend always doing a little internal audit of your mental state after you've done a physical thing, especially exercise and especially after eating a particular type of food.

Just see how you feel a few hours afterwards. I can tell you that after a long walk, my mental state is excellent and I sleep like a baby.

If you don't do anything else, you should take a walk every day."

Peak performance expert and coach Joseph Rodrigues on taking care of yourself to help others:

"Everyone I know that is really good at helping people take amazing care of themselves. They groom themselves really well.

They take care of their health and fitness. They surround themselves with things that they enjoy. They have a certain energy that is magnetic that makes people want to listen.

It is through the BEING that is uplifting, the words just carry the energy. The paradox: the more you care for yourself, the greater the capacity, energy and ability you have to care for someone else. If you know how to care for yourself, you can create that feeling of care."

The best leaders maximize their energy so they can energize others.

Don't overthink this.

It's not that complicated.

Don't wait.

Do it now.

PRINCIPLE #13:

Golden Moves

> *"The fundamentals are where your attention needs to be for the duration of your career."*
> -John Danaher, Brazilian Jiu Jitsu black belt

Self protection application

A "Golden Move" is a fundamental technique or practice that will work as a problem solver in many different situations.

You can think about a Golden Move as a metaphorical "Swiss Army Knife", one tool with multiple problem solving features.

The following are examples of Golden Moves in self protection:

1. Confident attitude. Confidence prevents an attack because when we have it, we look like the opposite of a victim or easy target. Confidence can help us overcome a violent attacker, because we believe that we can win and get home safely.

2. Fitness. If we are our best physical shape we look like less of a victim or easy target. Being in good physical shape can help us overcome a violent attacker, because we have built the strength and stamina to do so.

3. Fighters eyes. Good eyes can prevent a violent attack because if we continuously scan our environment, we can become aware of potential danger and avoid it before it happens. If we are attacked, good focused eyes allow us to see strikes coming and potentially avoid them, and also see opportunities for our own strikes to land.

4. The jab. A jab is a lead hand strike. It follows the "closest weapon, closest target" principle of Combatives expert Jim Grover. A jab can be used offensively to strike, offensively to distract, and defensively to disrupt. Bruce Lee called the jab the "Queen of Combat", because like in chess, it is the most versatile piece on the board. You will be very hard pressed to find a world champion fighter who doesn't have a great jab. A traditional jab in fighting is a closed fist strike where the knuckles hit the target. In self protection, you can also use your extended fingers to strike the eyes, or a c-hand strike to attack the throat. Strikes to the eyes and throat are illegal in sport fighting because they are vital targets that can cause permanent injury or even death. These types of strikes should only be used in life or death situations.

5. Dropping Energy. You can think about Dropping Energy as lowering your center of mass towards the ground. Your center of mass is found inside your body right around your belly button. You lower your center of mass by bending your knees, with your head positioned over your center of mass. By using Dropping Energy, you can both absorb force and generate force. If someone is pushing on you and you lower your center of mass, you can absorb their force

more effectively. If someone is pulling on your arm and you lower your center of mass, you can generate a counterforce more effectively. If someone is trying to pick you up off of the ground and you lower your center of mass, you can generate a counterforce more effectively. If you are throwing a strike and you lower your center of mass, you can generate force more effectively.

Keep it simple and work on your Golden Moves.

> *"Success in any endeavor (football medicine, marriage, parenting, leadership, rocket science, etc.) always comes down to about a half-dozen fundamentals. Then, narrow that down into your 2-3 vital functions and focus solely on those."*
>
> -Darren Hardy

Leadership application

There a few leadership practices that when repeated daily, over time can create staggering positive results. They can be found in my book "1% Warrior Leadership".

I put three of the most effective leadership Golden Moves into the "The Three Steps to Win The Day" formula:

1. ENERGIZE and prioritize your #1 Performance Enhancer. For most people, this is sleep.
2. Have ONE Three-Minute Magic Conversation per day. This is an uninterrupted, sincere conversation with one of

your team members where you are simply asking questions and listening.

3. UPGRADE Your Expertise for 15 minutes each day. Learn something new. This can come from books, podcasts, time with a mentor, etc.

There is also our 1% Warrior Goal Mastery System:

1. ONE goal.
2. ONE highest-impact activity to achieve your goal.
3. ONE habit to stop that is holding you back the most from achieving your goal.
4. ONE person that can help you the most in achieving your goal.

With the Win The Day and 1% Warrior systems, you now have seven high-leverage, high-impact leadership practices. They are all so easy to do that a twelve year old could do them.

When something is very easy to do, it is also just as easy NOT to do, because we are often looking for some "secret, complicated formula" that has been hidden from us all. There is no such thing.

These seven leadership Golden Moves are simple. So simple that they are often overlooked. We might think, "It can't be this simple. There's got to be more."

There isn't.

Don't overthink this.

It's not that complicated.

PRINCIPLE #14:

Don't Step Back Psychology

> *"We must have a superiority complex. Always attack. Never Surrender."*
> -General George Patton

Self protection application

When you have thoroughly exhausted every possibility of deescalation or escape, and you have no choice but to fight for your life, you must attack. You must go forward.

"Don't step back" psychology is the mindset that you will not be forced backwards once the fight has become physical.

You draw a "mental line" where your back foot is, and DECIDE that you will not be forced backward.

You will "attack your attacker". You become the predator, not the prey.

Legendary self protection expert Jim Grover says you need to "wear their shirt" and take up the space they just occupied by driving them backwards. You are "all over them".

Their are practical considerations as to why you should not move backwards, as you may trip over something behind you and end up on the ground. Humans also move forward much better than we move backwards.

If you are being pushed backwards by a bigger or stronger adversary, you can move laterally and circle to the left or right. Just don't step backwards.

"Don't Step Back" is just as much mental and emotional as it is physical. Before a situation becomes physical, you can and should try to talk the person out of violence. You can try to walk away or run away.

But if you have no choice but to fight, you must go forward.

> *"When Bear Bryant walked out on the football field, self-confidence hung in the air around him like a fine mist. That was good for at least one touchdown for Alabama. Confidence was a secret ingredient of Bryant's success, and Vince Lombardi's legend."*
>
> *-Joe Paterno*

Leadership application

Never show doubt.

Once a decision has been made and the mission has been set, you must never show doubt as a leader.

Never show doubt in the mission.

Never show doubt in your people.

Never show doubt in your organization.

And never show doubt in yourself.

If you have to, you can always adjust and make changes to the mission and tactics if new and better information becomes available that you did not have before. Be slow to decide the direction and mission, but be quick to pivot with new, solid information.

Be quick to admit mistakes as a leader. Correct them and move on. You will judged by your corrections far more than your mistakes. You won't be judged by the problems that arise. You'll be judged by how you handle them.

If you do have doubt, you can share it with a mentor, coach, or superior in the organization. Not family or friends. They don't need to hear it and be burdened with it.

Confidence is contagious. Unfortunately, doubt is much more contagious. It will spread through the organization like a virus if the CEO, president, head coach, etc. shows just an ounce of the stuff.

PRINCIPLE #15:

Hit Three Times Harder (Force Multipliers)

> *"Power is physical, emotional, and spiritual."*
> —Menamy Mitanes

Self protection application

In self protection training, we must always prepare for the worst case scenario. That is the attacker who is bigger, stronger, faster, and more skilled than us.

Learning to hit as hard as possible is a key component to defeating an attacker who has a real (or perceived) tactical advantage. The following are five keys putting every ounce of your power into your strikes.

1. Sit down

> *"If your center of gravity is just 10 centimeters lower, you will be able to generate three times stronger punch!"*
> —Tom Garland

Bend your knees while keeping your head over your center of gravity (your hips).

By "sitting down" in this manner, you are able to generate (and also absorb) much more force.

Self protection expert and "Guided Chaos" instructor Al Ridenhour explained this brilliantly on the Modern Combat and Survival Podcast:

"With the Dempsey Drop, when you drop your weight, because of inertia, the ground pushes back with equal force.

There is a plyometric effect taking place where there is a deceleration and acceleration of the muscles as the body attempts to stabilize itself from all that force from the drop as the ground pushes back with equal force.

If you time it right, you can actual channel that force or wave of energy coming back up for the ground as you strike. It creates an illusion. You are only moving a few inches, but you are penetrating with tremendous force like a sledgehammer.

This is what would people describe as "mystical energy" or the "death touch" in martial arts, but there is physics behind it."

2. Bodyweight as a weapon

> *"Exploding bodyweight is the most important weapon in fist-fighting or in boxing. Never forget that."*
> *-Jack Dempsey*

All power in striking comes from bodyweight transfer. It doesn't matter if the strike is a punch, kick, knee, elbow, head butt, etc. it is all a transfer of bodyweight that creates the powerful strike.

When you are throwing a strike, visualize launching your whole bodyweight into it, particularly your center of mass which is right around your bellybutton and a few inches inside of your body.

3. Attitude as a weapon

> *"Keep it fast, loose, and disrespectful. Combatives are 10 percent technique, 90 percent attitude. Movements are succinct, minimalist, and kind of ugly. We're pounding people."*
>
> *-Kelly McCann*

You must bring out your inner animal in a situation where your life or the life of someone you care about is at stake.

You must keep fighting with everything you've got not until your attacker is defeated, but until YOU are dead. That means that you give everything you've got until the very end. This is what will give you the best chance of survival.

This "animal attitude" is the number one reason why there are many stories of smaller people with no self protection training defeating much bigger and stronger attackers.

High respected self protection expert Kelly McCann describes this as: Rage with reason. Impact with attitude.

4. Hit through the target

> *"Think like a bullet."*
> *-Tim Larkin*

By "injecting" your strike into your attacker, it will feel much heavier and more powerful upon impact.

Boxing instructor Tom Garland describes this phenomenon beautifully in the article "How To Punch Harder" on the Extreme Strikers website:

"The goal is not to hit your opponent, you must hit a target which is 10-12 inches behind, beside or above your opponent, depending on the boxing technique. When you see the mitt, imagine your target is located behind the mitt if you target your straight punch. Punch the target behind the mitt. If you punch a punching bag, make sure to finish the impact behind the bag. Have you ever wondered why your punch doesn't have much power when you do everything properly? Here is the secret – your target is an imaginary object which is located near your opponent!"

5. Relax and explode

> *"A good martial artist does not become tense, but ready. Not thinking, yet not dreaming. Ready for whatever may come. The opponent expands, I contract. When he contracts, I expand. And when there is an opportunity, I do not hit; it hits all by itself."*
> *-Bruce Lee*

A powerful strike is not a push, but a "snap", like that at the end of whip.

I learned from MMA world heavyweight champion Fedor Emelianenko to visualize your fist as a "rock and the end of a rope", the rope being your arm. When you throw a rock tied to a rope, when the rock reaches the end of the rope, there will be a "snap".

Bodyweight transfer creates the power. Snap creates the concussive energy.

Russian Systema expert Menamy Mitanes on tension and relaxation:

"Tension is the mother of all evil. Tension prevents you from having a powerful strike. It works as a brake. When your emotions are high, you are weakened, and your power is taken away.

Fear and anger create tension. Being happy and enjoying the moment relaxes you, then you have more power because there is nothing stopping you, no tension.

Mike Tyson said, "There is nothing more deadly or more proficient than a happy fighter."

In summary, five keys to hitting as hard as possible:

1. Sit down
2. Bodyweight as a weapon
3. Attitude as a weapon
4. Hit through the target
5. Relax and explode

> "Passion fuels performance. If you don't love it, you'll never work hard enough to be great."
> -Gunnar Peterson

Leadership application

There are several "high leverage" mindsets and habits an organization can adopt that will serve as "force multipliers".

In military terms, a force multiplier is:

"A capability that, when added to and employed by a combat force, significantly increases the combat potential of that force and thus enhances the probability of successful mission accomplishment."

The following five force multipliers create an almost "unfair" competitive advantage for any organization on the planet when applied. And most of them cost little to nothing in dollars spent. Amazing.

1. Energy levels and enthusiasm

> "Motivation and energy levels have three times as much weight as physical resources."
> -Napoleon Bonaparte

A leader and organization that is motivated and energized by the work and the mission has a tremendous competitive advantage. Their energy is contagious to everyone around them.

According to retired Army 4-star General and former Secretary of State Colin Powell, "Optimism is a force multiplier."

2. Best People

> "A small team of A-players can run circles around a giant team of B and C-players."
> -Steve Jobs

Having a clear plan to attract, hire, and keep the best talent in your field is one of the simplest and most overlooked concepts in all of business.

According to performance expert and bestselling author Geoff Colvin:

"Bill Gates has said that if you took the twenty smartest people out of Microsoft it would be an insignificant company, and if you ask around the company what its core competency is, they don't say anything about software. They say it's hiring."

3. Speed wins

> "Success loves speed. Delay kills dreams."
> -Craig Ballantyne

Speed is a tremendous competitive advantage. Operating with just 10% more of a sense of urgency, compounded over time, leads to a tremendous gap between you and the competition.

World War 2 General George Patton's war philosophy:

"A good plan violently executed today is better than a perfect plan executed next week."

4. Upgrade your expertise

> *"Learn, learn, learn. The greatest competitive advantage is knowledge."*
> *-Mark Cuban*

There is more information out there that is easily accessible than any other time before in history. Books, audiobooks, podcasts, articles, spending time with a mentor or expert, etc.

99% of leaders won't take the time to spend an hour or two a day self-educating. Will you?

Bestselling author, investor, and business expert James Altucher proximity and success:

"Stand next to the smartest person in the room.

Harold Ramis did it (Bill Murray).

Steve Jobs did it (Steve Wozniak).

Craig Silverstein did it (Larry Page).

Kanye West did it (Jay-Z).

I make money only when I do this."

5. Leadership

> *"I'm always asked for what's the key to success in organizations. I always say the same thing. It's leadership. You want one thing, it's leadership. Great leaders make mediocre organizations fantastic. Poor leaders can kill the best of organizations."*
> *-Alan Weiss*

The number one force multiplier is a leader who:

Has energy and enthusiasm.

Surrounds themself with the best people.

Operates with a sense of urgency.

Never stops learning.

Don't overthink this.

It's not that complicated.

PRINCIPLE #16:

The BEST Defense

> *"Hitting the other guy before he hits you is the best kind of defense."*
> -Ramsey Dewey

Self protection application

The BEST defense is a good offense.

If you have no other choice but to fight to defend your life or the life of someone else, you must "go first". You must go animal and attack attack attack. You must switch the paradigm from being the prey to becoming the predator. Be first. Be ferocious.

Legendary Samurai Miyamoto Musashi had no concept of blocking and countering in his fighting system. He believed in preemptively striking first.

Combatives legend W.E. Fairbairn was a British Royal Marine and police officer. He developed a hand-to-hand combat system for the Shanghai Police at a time when it was one of the most dangerous cities in the world. He then went on to teach the allied special forces during World War II. He created his own fighting system known as Defendu. Fairbairn had no blocking or parrying in his Defendu system

> *"You can't win on defense. You can't win by blocking your way out of it."*
> *-Rory Miller*

Self protection situations are fast and furious, quick and dirty. They are not sport fights where there is a bell at the beginning of a timed round, an agreed upon rule set, and a referee and doctor standing by.

If you cannot run away or de-escalate, and you have no choice but to defend your life, attack first and keep going, keep going, keep going. As highly respected combatives instructor Lee Morrison says: "Me, me, more me". So you can go live to go home and hug the people you love.

> *"Success in war depends on the "golden rules of war": Speed, simplicity, and boldness."*
> *-General George Patton*

Leadership application

As a leader, you must do everything you can to stay in "Attack Mode".

People expect their leaders to be able to "wage war". They want their leaders to have the brains and the backbone to be capable of protecting them and winning.

Attack Mode is offensive and proactive. Defend Mode is defensive and reactive.

We want to aim to be in a proactive Attack Mode for at least 90% of our day. The other 10% will be reactionary to new challenges that arise, as organizations are dynamic and we can't predict every scenario or challenge in advance.

> *"I am an attacker, and my attack defends."*
> -Conor McGregor

Attack Mode:

Relentless solution focus

Continuous improvement mindset

Progress over perfection

Sense of urgency

Don't wait, do it now

Brief and bright communication

Simplicity (It's not that complicated)

Future focus

Positive focus

Certainty and enthusiasm

Focusing on your 1-2 Vital Functions

Working in the areas of your 1-2 Passionate Strengths

Growth initiatives for the organization

Leadership activities such as one-on-one conversations, managing by walking around, etc.

Defend Mode:

Mindless negativity of blame, excuses, venting, complaining, condemning

Focusing too much on problems instead of solutions.

Too much past focus

Focusing on the competition too much

Showing doubt

Broad focus (trying to do too much)

Focusing on trivial, low impact activities at the expense of your 1-2 Vital Functions

Drowning in ideas

Drowning in information

Drowning in opportunities

Paralyzed by perfection

In summary:

Visualize yourself as a lion. Stay in Attack Mode. It the absolute best thing you can do for your people and your organization.

PRINCIPLE #17:

The Water Balloon And The Ice Sculpture (Be Like Water)

> *"Be like water making its way through cracks. Do not be assertive, but adjust to the object, and you shall find a way around or through it. If nothing within you stays rigid, outward things will disclose themselves. Empty your mind, be formless. Shapeless, like water. If you put water into a cup, it becomes the cup. You put water into a bottle and it becomes the bottle. You put it in a teapot, it becomes the teapot. Now, water can flow or it can crash. Be water, my friend."*
>
> -Bruce Lee

Self protection application

In fighting, sometimes you need to be fluid like a water balloon. Other times you need to be solid like the ice sculpture.

Combatives are a continuous cycling of relaxation and explosion (tension), over and over again.

A counterintuitive secret of martial arts: the majority of time, you are relaxed and fluid like the water balloon.

If you stay tense or explosive the whole time, you will quickly fatigue. Continuous tension also clouds your ability to see and read your opponent. You won't be able to see the attacks coming as easily, or see opportunities for your own attacks.

In the avoidance and deescalation phase of a potentially violent encounter, if you are overly tense, you will not be able to think clearly to find the right words and make the right decisions that could potentially save your life.

Hall of Fame trainer Tom Yankello is widely recognized as one of the best boxing trainers in the world. He was the coach of six-time, four weight class, world champion Roy Jones Jr., and IBF lightweight world champion Paul Spadafora.

He has developed numerous champions & top contenders from beginner to the world championship level.

Yankello on relaxation:

"You have to be relaxed in boxing.

You absorb everything defensively when you are relaxed.

When you're in rhythm and you're relaxed, you'll be smooth.

Smooth is fast.

On the defensive end, you'll be soft.

On the offensive end, you'll be quicker.

And you'll be able to get in position smoother and quicker, and position beats speed."

> "I'm to the point now where if I get negativity from someone, I don't even respond back."
> -Andy Frisella

Leadership application

As a leader, you want to develop a "multi-dimensional personality".

You want to be able to stay calm during tense or crisis situations. The calmest one in the room is usually in the most control of any situation.

Warren Buffett on emotional control:

"You will continue to suffer if you have an emotional reaction to everything that is said to you.

True power is sitting back and observing things with logic.

True power is restraint.

If words control you, that means everyone else can control you.

Breathe and allow things to pass."

The other side of your multi-dimensional personality is the ability to be honest and direct and challenge others to be better when necessary.

An excerpt from the instant classic leadership book "Radical Candor" by Kim Scott:

"Colin Powell once remarked that being responsible sometimes means pissing someone off. You have to accept that sometimes people on your team will be mad at you. In fact, if nobody is ever mad at you, you probably aren't challenging your team enough."

In summary: Develop a multi-dimensional leadership personality. Have the ability to stay calm and fluid, and an equal ability to be honest and direct when necessary.

PRINCIPLE #18:

Splatter Factor

> *"Techniques fail. Focus on principles and keep going!"*
> *-Sal Mascoli, ret. United States Marine and law enforcement officer*

Self protection application

Real fights are not smooth and sequential and clean like you see in the movies. They are messy, dirty, and scary. This is the "Splatter Factor". There are no foolproof, 100% "guaranteed to work" techniques. The most important thing is that you keep going, keep moving, and keep fighting until you've given every last ounce of your energy and breath.

Because of the unpredictability and chaos of the fight, we want to focus on principles over techniques.

Five Simple Principles That Can Save Your Life:

1. Be First. If you have no other option but to fight, attack first. Use the art of surprise to catch the opponent off guard.

2. Go Animal. Attack above the neck. Attack the vital targets of the face, eyes, neck, throat, jaw, temples, and back of the head over and over again.

3. Hard Weapons Against Soft Targets. Use the your hard weapons (fingers, hands, fists, forearms, elbows, knees, shins, feet, etc.) against the soft targets above the neck.

4. Don't Step Back Psychology. Once you have no choice but to fight, keep attacking and attacking and attacking like a buzzsaw. Keep moving forward.

5. Don't Stop. Don't stop attacking your attacker until you are dead. Don't stop fighting until you are able to go home safely.

Fights are fast and messy and dirty and ugly. You probably will not be able to remember specific techniques. But if you can remember to do things like "Go Animal", and "Don't Stop", you will dramatically increase your odds of winning and surviving.

> *"It's better to be in motion ignorantly than static intelligently. Ignorance on fire is better than knowledge on ice."*
> *-Sean Smith*

Leadership application

Done is better than perfect. Sometimes good enough is good enough. Progress over perfection. Once you have 80% of the information, make a decision and go. Don't overthink this. It's not that complicated.

There are 88 keys on a piano. Peak performance expert and coach Jason Capital on the "89th Key":

"The 89th Key Delusion:

Everyone is seeking the 89th key, that magical mythical secret ingredient and formula, and when they find it, they I'll be successful.

There is no 89th key. If there is a magical formula, an 89th key, here it is: The Key is inside of you.

As long as you keep going, you cannot fail. But if you stop at any point, you lose. It is that simple.

Stop wasting time looking for magical information that doesn't exist. Instead, commit to doing the work and keep going."

Tim Grover, peak performance expert and author of the brilliant book "Relentless", on trusting yourself:

"Can you be reasonably successful by just following directions and staying within the lines? Sure. That's what most people do.

But if we're talking about being elite, if you want to be unstoppable, you have to learn to put aside everything you've been taught, all the restrictions and limitations, the negativity and doubt. If that sounds complicated and confusing, let me make it simple: You have to stop thinking.

It's so basic. Are you good at what you do? Maybe even great at what you do? Can you be the best? Yes? If you said no, I'll give you a moment to change your answer. Again: Can you be the best? Of course you can. Then why are you still questioning your ability to do it?

Quick answer: because at some point, you made something simple into something complicated, and you stopped trusting yourself."

In summary:

Stay in motion.

Keep moving.

Action over perfection.

Stop thinking.

Act your way into it.

Keep it simple.

Just do it.

Results will come.

PRINCIPLE #19:

No Guarantees

> *"Techniques fail. Principles don't fail. Keep things simple."*
> —Jim Grover

Self protection application

There are no guarantees in self protection situations. No matter how strong, fit, and well trained you are, there are no guarantees that you will defeat your attacker. There are simply too many variables.

Does the attacker have a weapon?

Is your attacker better trained than you?

Does he have accomplices waiting in the shadows to sneak up behind you?

Do you slip on the terrain and injure yourself?

Do you you injure yourself in the initial flurry of the fight?

Do you win the fight, but by doing so face serious legal or financial consequences in the aftermath?

Etc.

There is only one guaranteed technique in combatives:

Distance. Don't be there in the first place.

The only way to truly "win" a street fight is to not fight at all.

This is why avoidance is our most important pillar.

Don't overthink this.

There are no guarantees in self protection.

Don't be there in the first place.

> "I did one thing to be number one in my market as a vice president at 25 years old. I recruited better. I brought more people into the firm that succeeded than anyone else. Everything else about the job I didn't care about."
> -Gary Keller

Leadership application

There are no guarantees in business or life. It doesn't matter how great your product is or how hard you work. There are no guarantees for success. There are simply too many variables.

New competition.

Political changes.

New governmental regulations.

A global pandemic.

Changes in customer tastes.

New trends.

Etc.

The closest things you will get to guarantees in business are this:

1. Surround yourself with the best and brightest people you can. The best team members, the best mentors and advisors, the best friends and colleagues, read the best books, etc. This will allow you to learn faster and also solve problems

faster than your competition. In order to make this work, you must be an EXPERT listener.

2. Model success. Success leaves clues. Study the most successful individuals and organizations in your field, as well as those in other fields. Take the best practices, then put them into action.

Here's a story about the founder of Walmart told by Navid Amin:

"Sam Walton was infamous for studying what his competition was doing right so that he could implement these strengths in his own stores.

In the early days, he would have store managers walk through other discount stores memorizing as many prices as they could, writing them down as soon as they walked out of the store.

Some managers would even wait until stores closed at night and look through their trash bins to find out what they were pricing their products at.

Sam didn't stop at that—any vacation or family camping trip was an opportunity for Sam to look at stores.

By doing so, he was able to accumulate the best practices of stores all around the world into one store."

Surround yourself with the best and brightest people you can.

Model success.

No guarantees, but these two simple practices will increase your odds of succeeding dramatically.

Don't overthink this.

It's not that complicated.

PRINCIPLE #20:

Keep Showing Up (Keep Training)

> *"Nobody cares. Work harder. Keep hammering."*
> *-Cameron Hanes*

Self protection application

If you want to put yourself in the best position to be able to defend your life or the lives of people you care about the most, you have to keep showing up.

Showing up where?

To the gym.

Why?

To get comfortable with being uncomfortable.

A life or death struggle is the most uncomfortable thing imaginable.

But if you make yourself uncomfortable every day, you'll be much more comfortable with discomfort if a terrible violent situation ever arises.

The best ways I have found to make yourself uncomfortable on a daily basis:

1. Martial arts training. The best training for self defense is mixed martial arts training with the added study and practice of:

Recognizing pre-assault cues

Verbal deescalation

Verbal assertiveness

Awareness and avoidance skills

Animal mindset

Attacking vital targets with techniques illegal in sport fighting

Mixed martial arts training is mainly composed of boxing, Muay Thai kickboxing, Brazilian Jiu Jitsu, wrestling, and judo.

If I could pick two disciplines to start with, it would be Brazilian Jiu Jitsu and boxing.

2. Tactical strength and conditioning work with a reputable and knowledgeable trainer. Metabolic circuits are an outstanding choice.

3. Assertiveness. This is standing up for yourself. This is not allowing mistreatment to go unchecked and unaddressed.

4. Make the hard choice. Examples: taking the stairs instead of the elevator, choosing the chicken instead of the cheeseburger, taking 100% responsibility for things instead of blaming, saying no to things that don't bring you joy or growth, having the difficult conversation instead of putting it off, etc.

"Difficult conversations" are having the uncomfortable conversations with family, friends, coworkers, your boss, etc. that most people would put off because they are hard to do. They are conversations, not confrontations, and we always let people keep their dignity.

Keep training your mind and body on a daily basis to be comfortable with discomfort.

Over time, the results will be incredible, and you will see a great positive change in your life as a whole.

> *"Here's to those unknown and thankless hours, days, months and years of lonely hardship. What you do onstage belongs to the world; but those countless hours of unwitnessed and unappreciated preparation are yours and yours alone. They, not the stage, represent your true character."*
>
> -John Danaher

Leadership application

As a leader, you must keep showing up. There are no days off. You must be able to not just show up, but to show up with energy and enthusiasm. Especially on the days you don't feel like it.

One of the absolute true tests of a leader: Can you energize your team even when you don't feel like it?

Pioneering industrialist Andrew Carnegie only had two criteria when hiring managers/leaders: can they energize themselves and can they energize others.

You must keep showing up and giving your best effort, whatever it is that day. It will change day to day. Some days you'll be more tired, stressed, or even a little sick.

What matters is that you give your best effort for that day.

Tom Cruise's life mantra: "Just do the best you can. All I can do every day is do the best I can. And learn."

You must keep showing up with consistency. Consistency over intensity.

David Meltzer formerly served as CEO of the renowned Leigh Steinberg Sports & Entertainment agency, which was the inspiration for the movie Jerry Maguire.

His life's mission is to empower over 1 billion people to be happy. He is a three-time international best-selling author and a Top 100 Business Coach.

Here is a simple formula for success from David:

"You have to work hard, smart, and long.

You have to enjoy the consistent, persistent pursuit of your potential.

I make people I work with promise me they are going to stick to it.

What's going to happen is you'll be 30 years old and 25% of the way there, and you're going to quit like 99% of the people on earth.

Here's what's sad: if you would last another five years to age 35, there would be even more pressure on you.

All your friends will call you loser and your parents would be more disappointed in you.

At 35 years old you're 50% of the way there, but 99.9% of the people quit.

That leaves the 1% of the 1%.

And now 2 1/2 years later at age 37 1/2, you're 100% of the way there.

And 1 3/4 years later, your 200% there.

7/8 of the year, your 400%.

7/16 you're 800%.

That's how Bezos made 100 billion dollars.

Through believing in himself and consistency. He understands the enjoyment of the consistent, persistent pursuit of his potential."

In summary, keep showing up.

Keep showing up with energy.

Keep showing up with your best effort, whatever it is that day.

And keep showing up consistently.

Don't overthink this.

It's not that complicated.

You've got this.

PRINCIPLE #21:

Iron Sharpens Iron (Find The Best People)

> *"You are the average of the five people you spend the most time with. Show me your friends and I'll show you your future."*
> —Jim Rohn

Self protection application

Surround yourself with the best and brightest.

In martial arts training, your coaching and training partners are very important. Iron sharpens iron. It is crucial to have great people around you to make you better.

The best investment you can ever make is in yourself. The more you invest in yourself, the more you can help others. Hire the best martial arts coaches and strength and conditioning trainers that you CANNOT afford. That means that you may have to sacrifice in other areas of your life and the things that you spend money on. Train at the best martial arts gyms and fitness centers possible. Find the best training partners you can. The best training partners are positive, safe, reliable, skillful, and committed to continuous improvement.

According to Jeff Olson, author of "The Slight Edge":

"Your income will tend to be the average of your ten best friends' incomes. Do you know why birds of a feather flock together? Because they're all going in the same direction. They share a common vision. It's called the Law of Association. It's a Law because it always works."

Surround yourself with the best people you can. You become the average of the people you spend the most time with.

If you want to be a great martial artist, surround yourself with great martial artists.

If you want to be more positive, spend more time with positive people.

If you want to be more confident, spend more time with confident people.

If you want to be healthier, spend more time with healthy people.

If you want to be more successful, spend more time with successful people.

And if you want to be happier, spend more time with happy people.

Don't overthink this.

It's not that complicated.

> "Who you are is who you attract. That is the law of magnetism. If you want to attract better people, become the kind of person you desire to attract."
> -John C. Maxwell

Leadership application

As a leader, you must be the kind of person you want to attract onto your team and into your organization.

If you want to attract positive team members, you must be positive.

If you want to attract focused team members, you must be focused.

If you want to attract energized team members, you must be energized.

And if you want to attract high integrity team members, you must be high integrity.

In everything in life, 95% of success is in the set up.

In leadership, creating an organization that performs at a world-class level can be boiled down to two things:

1. Create a big, bold, enormous vision.
2. Create an environment and culture that attracts, develops, and keeps the best of the best people in your field.

World class starts with you as a leader. Be the type of leader that attracts the best people.

Don't overthink this.

It's not that complicated.

PRINCIPLE #22:

Ten Minutes With A Mentor (Find The Best Coaches)

> "You can't be what you can't see. You must get exposed to the quality you want to have."
> -Jay Shetty

Self protection application

Ten minutes with a world class mentor or coach can be worth more than ten years with good instructor.

You'll learn more spending time with a world class mentor or coach than you will reading 100 books.

Surround yourself with the best mentors and coaches you possibly can. It is one of the only true shortcuts to success, and it is by far the most powerful.

When you ask the right questions to the right person, a whole new world will open up for you. You must do everything you can to expose yourself to the masters of your craft. Listen to everything they say, and model what they do.

As Pablo Picasso once said: "Good artists copy. Great artists steal."

Modeling in itself can save you ten to twenty years of time on your journey to greatness.

> "The best piece of advice I ever received: Ignore 99 out of 100 people. But when you find that 1 person, listen to everything they say."
> -Tai Lopez

Leadership application

Show me your heroes, I'll show you your future.

Who are your leadership heroes?

Read their books and biographies. Listen to their interviews and speeches. And if possible, meet them in person.

Spend as much time as possible with people who are five to fifty years ahead of you at where you want to be. If you ask, they'll tell you exactly what you need to do, and equally as important, they'll tell you exactly what not to waste your time on.

Model the masters.

Model their daily habits, the books they read, and study their personal models and mentors.

A story from Brian Tracy, the legendary world-renowned peak performance expert and author of "Maximum Achievement":

"M.R. Kop Kopmeyer spent more than 50 years studying success.

He derived more than 1,000 success principles from around 6,000 books.

The most important principle of all: Use proven success methods.

Learn from the experts.

Successful people are those who learn from others who have gone before them.

Unsuccessful people are those that try to make it all up.

Successful people follow proven success principles, proven formulas, and they do them over and over again until they master them."

Don't overthink this.

It's not that complicated.

Success leaves clues for the few who take the time to really look.

PRINCIPLE #23:

Weaponize Your Instincts

> *"Caveman Vs Scientist: Sometimes you have to be a scientist and sit back and think, and sometimes you have to be a caveman, bite down on your mouthpiece, and outwill the other person."*
> —Daniel Bohigian, Brazilian Jiu Jitsu Black Belt

Self protection application

In the initial physical flurry and tornado of a violent situation where you must defend yourself, I can promise you that there is not much thinking going on.

You will go on autopilot, and four things will come out:

1. The simple techniques that you've trained
2. Gross motor skills
3. Your primal inclinations and natural tendencies
4. Your strength and fitness

Why not train all of those things together?

1. Train a dozen or so simple techniques over and over and over again, not until you can do them right, but until you cannot do them wrong.

2. Gross motor skills use the large muscles in the body and include broader movements such as pushing, pulling, swinging your arms, and running.

Fine motor skills are those that require a high degree of precision and control in the small muscles of the hand (such as writing or an advanced wrist lock attack).

Don't train complicated, multiple-step techniques for self defense. It is unlikely you'll be able to execute them under duress.

3. Figure out which techniques and positions come most naturally to you. These are the techniques that you learn quicker than other techniques, you revert back to them more often, and your instructor notices that you do them very well.

4. Practice your techniques against a resisting opponent as a component of your training. This is called sparring, and it will allow you to get technical work as well as strength and conditioning work at the same time.

Don't overthink this.

It's not that complicated.

Now go train.

> *"A billionaire appears to be someone who is a master at everything. But, in truth, they're specialists in one or a few areas and average or subpar at everything else. So, how do they get so much done? Leverage! They do what they do best and get others to do the rest."*
>
> *-Paul C. Brunson*

Leadership application

Figure out what your biggest strengths are as a leader. Examples:
- Public speaking
- One-on-one conversations
- Media relations
- Writing
- Reading and researching
- Energizing the team by walking around and talking to small groups and individuals
- Sales
- Marketing
- Finance
- Product development
- Customer service
- Strategy

Narrow it down to your two biggest strengths, and double down on them.

Match them up with the two vital functions of the organization, the two things that drive results the most, and you will have mega-success.

Peak performance expert and bestselling author of "Tools Of Titans" Tim Ferriss on this phenomena:

"The superheroes you have in mind (titans, icons, billionaires) are nearly all walking flaws who have maximized 1-2 strengths."

Lock in on the two things that you do best as a leader that also make the biggest positive impact on your organization. Aim to do those two things for 90% of your day. Keep it simple, because simple works.

PRINCIPLE #24:

White Belt Mentality (Never Stop Learning)

> *"I always knew I'd be successful because I knew I worked harder than anyone else. What I lacked in talent, I'd make up for with tenacity and learning."*
> -Criss Angel

Self protection application

No matter how much experience and knowledge you have, always show up with a willingness to listen and learn.

A White Belt Mentality is having a "beginners mind".

There is always more to learn if you keep your mind open.

Chad Lyman is a Las Vegas police officer, Brazilian Jiu Jitsu Black Belt, and head grappling instructor at Extreme Couture (one of the most respected mixed martial arts academies in the world). He has a simple training rule that has served him well:

"The rule of three:

If you go three minutes without air, you will probably die. If you lose more than 3 pints of blood, you will probably die. If you go three days in the desert without shelter or water, you will probably die.

I tell myself that if I don't train in a three day period, I'm going to die.

That might only be for 15 minutes that day. I don't have a three day period in my life when I don't train.

That's beyond strength and conditioning, that is separate. This is training with an unwilling, uncooperative opponent. That is where you really start setting yourself up to do well."

As much of an expert as Chad Lyman is, he still prioritizes showing up regularly with the mindset of learning and improving.

> *"One hour per day of study will put you at the top of your field within three years. Within five years you'll be a national authority. In seven years, you can be one of the best people in the world at what you do."*
>
> *-Earl Niahtinaale*

Leadership application

Out of the 500-plus leadership principles, habits, and tactics that I know, continuous learning is in the top-five highest impact of them all.

Leaders are learners.

Leaders are readers.

And knowledge is the biggest competitor advantage.

If we asked 100 leaders right now, "how many of you are self-educating to improve your leadership ability for at least 15 minutes on a daily basis?", you'll be surprised to find that it is 5 or less.

This is an opportunity for a leader to gain a tremendous competitive advantage if they can simply fully commit to continuous learning.

It could be from:

- Books
- Audiobooks
- Podcasts
- Documentaries
- Mentors
- Coaches
- Articles
- Seminars
- Etc.

It's not how you get the information that is important. It's that you take in the best information that you possibly can on a consistent basis.

Not all books, podcasts, mentors, etc. are created equal. Strive to learn from the absolute best of the best in your field.

Keep showing up with a White Belt Mentality.

Don't overthink this.

It's not that complicated.

CONCLUSION:

Don't Be There

> *"All I want to know is where I'm going to die so I don't go there."*
> -Charlie Munger, billionaire partner at Berkshire Hathaway

If you only remember one thing from this book it is this: Don't be there. Be aware of where serious problems and bad things happen, and avoid those places at all cost.

Don't overthink this.

It's not that complicated.

99.9% of self protection is the awareness and avoidance of violence. Life a safe lifestyle. You already know how to do this. A safe lifestyle:

Ask yourself, "What advice would I give to someone I care about that would keep them safe?" Take that same advice for yourself.

Always trust your gut. It is never wrong. If something feels wrong about a person or situation, avoid it and get away as fast as you can.

Have the mentality that no one is coming to save you. You must be your own personal security team.

Rely on nothing and rely on no one. You must take 100% responsibility for your own safety.

Lock your doors at all times, not just at night.

Have a home security system.

Don't drive aggressively.

Avoid bad places.

Avoid being alone in bad places.

Etc.

You already know how to do this.

> *"The essence of strategy is choosing what not to do."*
> *-Michael Porter*

One of best things you can ever do as a leader is figure what things will destroy the success of your organization, and avoid them at all costs. If you can simply do that, you'll be ahead of almost everyone.

Don't overthink this.

It's not that complicated.

Some of the biggest things to avoid as a leader:

1. Hiring the wrong people.
2. Promoting the wrong people to leadership positions.
3. Demotivating motivated people.
4. Talking when you should be listening.

Bestselling author and peak performance expert Tim Ferriss proposes a brilliant question: "What if I could only subtract to solve problems? What should I put on my not-to-do list?"

Awareness and avoidance. Don't be there.

Stay 1% Warrior. Stay in motion. Progress over perfection. 1% better than yesterday.

Leadership is the answer. Your people are counting on you.

Stay safe out there. The people you care about the most are counting on you.

24 Principles Of Self Protection Summaries

PILLAR ONE: AWARENESS AND AVOIDANCE
PRINCIPLE #1 BE YOUR OWN PROTECTOR

"The true secret is to never be dependent on anything. Once you're dependent, you will always have insecurity." Firas Zahabi

Self protection application

When facing a situation where you must defend your life, you must have the mentality that no one is coming to save you. You must be your own personal security team.

"One of the greatest things you can do in your life is become your own best friend."
-Joseph Rodrigues

Leadership application:

No one is coming to turn you into a better leader. Take 100% responsibility for becoming the best leader you can be. Self educate. Read and study great leadership. Seek out coaches and mentors who you can not only learn from, but who will tell you your blind spots and where you can improve.

PRINCIPLE #2 DON'T BE THERE

"It is remarkable how much long-term advantage people like us have gotten by trying to be consistently not stupid, instead of trying to be very intelligent."
-Charlie Munger, billionaire partner at Berkshire Hathaway

Self protection application:
99.9% of self protection is the awareness and avoidance of violence. Ask yourself, "What advice would I give to someone I care about that would keep them safe?" Take that same advice for yourself. Life a safe lifestyle. You already know how to do this.

"One of the greatest ways to avoid trouble is to keep it simple."
-Charlie Munger

Leadership application:
99.9% of success is in the setup.
A big component of successful setup as a leader is avoidance:
Avoid hiring the wrong people.
Avoid promoting the wrong person into a leadership position.
Avoid the wrong business partnership.
Avoid working for the wrong person or company.
Avoid focusing on the wrong things in the business.
Avoid starting the wrong business.
Avoid bad business investments.

PRINCIPLE #3 SHEEPDOG MENTALITY

> *"Competence, caring, and conviction combine to form a fundamental element shaping the fighting spirit of your troops."*
> -Jim Mattis, ret. General U.S. Marines

Self-protection application
Pat McNamara, retired Delta Force operator, on staying sheepdog: "You are the agent in charge of your own executive protection detail. Your loved ones are counting on you. Remember why you are staying fit, staying smart, and keeping your skills up. Stay sheepdog."

> *"Safety is the single most important piece of foundation needed for great culture."*
> -Daniel Coyle, The Culture Code

Leadership application
Put the success and happiness of your team before your own.
Make those who follow you feel safe.
Practiced heart-centered listening. Let them know that their opinions and feelings are respected and valued. Let them them know that they will not be punished for having opinions that are different than yours.
Protect your team members from mistreatment from co-workers, managers, and those outside of your organization.
Have the courage to stand up for your people.

PILLAR TWO: ATTITUDE
PRINCIPLE #4 ATTITUDE IS A WEAPON

> *"Marines believe that attitude is a weapon system."*
> -General Jim Mattis

Self protection application

People with confident attitudes make hard targets. If you carry yourself with mental, emotional, and physical confidence in your everyday life, you will find for the most part that people will simply leave you alone.

> *"Your confidence level determines your life."*
> -Dre Baldwin

Leadership application

Leadership Confidence = Certainty and Enthusiasm

As a leader, your attitude of "Certainty and Enthusiasm" is a weapon against mediocrity and unhappiness in your team and in your organization.

You must "bring the juice" every day. The juice is that energy of Certainty and Enthusiasm that is contagious to everyone around you.

PRINCIPLE #5 NEVER SEE YOURSELF ON THE LOSING SIDE OF VIOLENCE

> *"I often tell my clients that visualization is like bringing a gun to a knife fight: your previously negative thoughts and self-talk won't stand a chance against the more powerful detailed visions of success you are about to create."*
> -Dr. Jason Selk

Self protection application

When you are thinking about what a violent encounter where you must defend your life or someone else's, never imagine yourself on the losing end. This is bad programming. You are programming yourself to fail.

The mind can't tell the difference between "mental rehearsal" and the real life thing.

> *"Physical dominance can make you great. Mental dominance is what ultimately will make you unstoppable."*
> -Tim Grover, author of "Relentless"

Leadership application

Be the "chief visionary" to your team and organization. As the late Steve Jobs said, you must "project the future".

Never see your team members or organization failing. Instead, see a positive vision of the future in your mind. Visualize your past triumphs. See yourself, your team, and your organization as the best version it can be. Imagine yourself, your team, and your organization achieving your dream goal.

Over-communicate that positive vision over and over again to all your team members. Never show doubt in the vision.

PRINCIPLE #6 MENTAL, EMOTIONAL, AND PHYSICAL POSTURE

> *"Get your act together. Stand up straight with your shoulders back. It's a powerful position because it means you're brave enough to take what's coming."*
> *-Dr. Jordan Peterson*

Self protection application

Strong posture = hard target.
Poor posture = easy target.
One of the easiest ways to avoid violence is not to look, act, think, and talk like a victim. To think and do the opposite of what a victim thinks and does.

> *"Research shows that attitudes follow behavior – if we act in a certain way, over time our attitudes follow. The emotions you express, such as confidence or happiness, are contagious –they influence those around you."*
> *-Jeffrey Pfeffer*

Leadership application

People want to follow those who have a strong physical, mental, and emotional posture. Strong posture is equated to confidence. Confidence is equated to good leadership.

Strong posture and leadership confidence comes from putting in the repetitions to achieve expertise. It comes from positive self talk and positive visualization.

It comes from doing the right things. Legally, equitably, ethically. It comes from giving your best effort every day, especially when you don't feel like it. Work to develop your strong posture and leadership confidence every day.

PRINCIPLE #7 THE POWER OF NO

Self protection application

> *"No" is a word that must never be negotiated, because the person who chooses not to hear it is trying to control you...Declining to hear "no" is a signal that someone is either seeking control or refusing to relinquish it."*
> —Gavin de Becker

"No" is a complete sentence.
You can exercise your "no muscle" every day.
Say no to mistreatment.
Say no to those who waste your time and drain your energy.
Say no to those who don't want the best for you.
Say NO to someone who wants to hurt you or people you care about.
By exercising your "no muscle" every day, you will be far more capable of bringing out your "Power of No" when you need it the most.
Your voice is a powerful weapon. In a situation where someone is trying to bring you physical harm, you must be able to say "NO" so loud and clear so that person feels your righteous anger and defiance from every single cell of your body.

"When we say no, after the initial, short-term annoyance, disappointment, or anger of the other person wears off, the respect kicks in. When we push back effectively, it shows people that your time is highly valuable. It distinguishes the professional from the amateur."
-Greg McKeown

Leadership application

Saying "yes" is a tremendous time waster.

We must learn to say no to the things that don't get us closer to our most important goals.

We must learn to say no to spending time with people who do not bring us joy or growth.

We must say no to the negative thoughts and limiting beliefs that hold us back.

We must say no to the distractions that do not allow us to best share our special gifts, thus benefiting the world around us.

PRINCIPLE #8 CAPABLE OF CRUELTY

> *"Stand up for yourself like a respectable human being and be a little bit of a light on the world instead of a blight."*
> *-Dr. Jordan Peterson*

Self protection application

We must take the following mental, physical, and emotional posture:

"I am kind and respectful, but do not cross me. Because if you cross me and mistreat me, I will make it very uncomfortable for you."

We must be capable of cruelty. That does not mean that we use this cruelty every day. We only need to use it if we are under attack mentally, emotionally, or physically.

> *"It's not what you preach. It's what you tolerate."*
> *-Jocko Willink, ret Navy SEAL commander*

Leadership application

As a leader, you must be able to challenge people directly, and never walk by mediocrity without addressing it. For our leadership purposes, we will define "cruelty" as the following:

Tough love, straightforward honesty, constructive feedback, directness without removing the dignity of the receiver.

PRINCIPLE #9 DO THE SINGLE HARDEST THING (GET COMFORTABLE WITH DISCOMFORT)

"Making yourself uncomfortable speeds up the process of mental toughness."
-Dr. Jason Selk

Self defense application

Do something that makes you uncomfortable every day.
By doing this, you are mentally, physically, and emotionally preparing yourself for if you ever have to defend your life against an attacker
Ask yourself this in any situation:
What's the single hardest thing I can do?
Do that.

"If you are ever at the crossroads of making a difficult decision, always ask yourself, "What is the hard choice?". Then take that path."
-Jerzy Gregorek

Leadership application

Your success and happiness in life and leadership will be determined by the number of difficult things you do in a week.
The number of difficult conversations you have.
The extra time you spend reading and educating yourself instead of going out with friends on the weekend.

The going to the gym five days a week to keep your energy up so you can energize others.

The admitting when you made a mistake.

Make the hard choice every day. Your people will see this and respect you more for it.

PRINCIPLE #10 LET PEOPLE KEEP THEIR DIGNITY (VERBAL DE-ESCALATION AND DIFFUSION)

"Most people don't want to fight that badly."
-John Danaher

Self protection application
In a social violence situation, most people want you to talk them out of the fight. If you can show them respect and let them keep their pride and dignity, most people will walk away without trying to fight you.

"Converse, don't confront."
-Jim Ross

Leadership application
You will have to have many difficult conversations as a leader. It may be with a team member, your boss, a co-worker, a business partner, etc.
When having frank conversations, it is absolutely possible to have discourse without disrespect.
Conversation without confrontation. To do this, you must first do everything you can to remove your emotions from the situation. I prefer any difficult conversation to be done one-on-one whenever possible. It allows both parties to speak more freely and keep their dignity.
There are exceptions to this. Sometimes you need a witness for legal purposes, or someone else in the room for safety purposes.

PRINCIPLE #11 ALWAYS TRUST YOUR GUT

> *"We must learn and then teach our children that niceness does not equal goodness. Niceness is a decision, a strategy of social interaction; it is not a character trait. People seeking to control others almost always present the image of a nice person in the beginning."*
> -Gavin de Becker

Self protection application

If something feels wrong about a person or situation, get out of there without hesitation.

We all have an incredible sense of intuition that we are born with. Unfortunately, we do not always choose to listen to it. That internal protector is always switched on, ready to sound the alarm on dangerous situations. It is one of the most important and underrated aspects of self protection. Always trust your gut and always trust your feelings.

> *"Pay attention to whom your energy increases and decreases around, because that's the universe giving you a hint of who you should embrace or stray from."*
> -Wesley Snipes

Leadership application

Train yourself every day to listen to your intuition, no matter how softly it may speak. It is constantly giving you feedback. Always trust that gut intuition. It is never wrong.

PILLAR THREE: ANIMAL
PRINCIPLE #12 FITNESS IS A WEAPON (STRONGER PEOPLE ARE HARDER TO KILL)

> *"As a police officer in Miami, at least once in your career, your physical fitness will determine whether you live or die."*
> -Tony Sentmanat, retired SWAT team officer

Self protection application
Defending you life against an attacker is an athletic endeavor. It requires speed, strength and stamina, just like any other sport. You don't have to work on this for 15 hours a week like a professional athlete or bodybuilder. You simply want to be in YOUR best shape in the limited amount of time that you have to train.

> *"No one who is operating at an elite level long-term is ignoring their health—in business or life. Physical fitness is not just about being ripped or strong; it is about having the energy needed to lead."*
> -Jason Redman, ret. Navy SEAL

Leadership application
Maximize your energy in order to energize others. The ability to energize others is absolutely crucial to your effectiveness as a leader. Doing the right kind of physical exercise on a regular basis is a key component to maximizing your energy.

The right kind of exercise:
1. You feel energized when you're done with the workout
2. Your risk of injury is low
3. You enjoy the type of training you're doing
4. You enjoy the people you are doing it with

The right kind of exercise can be done in as little as fifteen to thirty minutes per day, five days per week.

PRINCIPLE #13 GOLDEN MOVES

"The fundamentals are where your attention needs to be for the duration of your career."
-John Danaher, Brazilian Jiu Jitsu black belt

Self protection application
A "Golden Move" is a fundamental technique or practice that will work as a problem solver in many different situations.
You can think about a Golden Move as a metaphorical "Swiss Army Knife", one tool with multiple problem solving features.

"Success in any endeavor (football medicine, marriage, parenting, leadership, rocket science, etc.) always comes down to about a half-dozen fundamentals. Then, narrow that down into your 2-3 vital functions and focus solely on those."
-Darren Hardy

Leadership application
There a few leadership practices that when repeated daily, over time can create staggering positive results. They can be found in my book "1% Warrior Leadership".
I put three of the most effective leadership Golden Moves into the "The Three Steps to Win The Day" formula:
1. ENERGIZE and prioritize your #1 Performance Enhancer. For most people, this is sleep.

2. Have ONE Three-Minute Magic Conversation per day. This is an uninterrupted, sincere conversation with one of your team members where you are simply asking questions and listening.

3. UPGRADE Your Expertise for 15 minutes each day. Learn something new. This can come from books, podcasts, time with a mentor, etc.

PRINCIPLE #14 DON'T STEP BACK PSYCHOLOGY

"We must have a superiority complex. Always attack. Never Surrender."
-General George Patton

Self protection application
When you have thoroughly exhausted every possibility of deescalation or escape, and you have no choice but to fight for your life, you must attack. You must go forward.

"Don't step back" psychology is the mindset that you will not be forced backwards once the fight has become physical.

You draw a "mental line" where your back foot is, and DECIDE that you will not be forced backward.

You will "attack your attacker". You become the predator, not the prey.

"When Bear Bryant walked out on the football field, self-confidence hung in the air around him like a fine mist. That was good for at least one touchdown for Alabama. Confidence was a secret ingredient of Bryant's success, and Vince Lombardi's legend."
-Joe Paterno

Leadership application
Never show doubt.

Once a decision has been made and the mission has been set, you must never show doubt as a leader.

Never show doubt in the mission.
Never show doubt in your people.
Never show doubt in your organization.
And never show doubt in yourself.

PRINCIPLE #15 HIT THREE TIMES HARDER (FORCE MULTIPLIERS)

> *"Power is physical, emotional, and spiritual."*
> *-Menamy Mitanes*

Self protection application

In self protection training, we must always prepare for the worst case scenario. That is the attacker who is bigger, stronger, faster, and more skilled than us.

Learning to hit as hard as possible is a key component to defeating an attacker who has a real (or perceived) tactical advantage.

> *"Passion fuels performance. If you don't love it, you'll never work hard enough to be great."*
> *-Gunnar Peterson*

Leadership application

There are several "high leverage" mindsets and habits an organization can adopt that will serve as "force multipliers".

In military terms, a force multiplier is:

"A capability that, when added to and employed by a combat force, significantly increases the combat potential of that force and thus enhances the probability of successful mission accomplishment."

PRINCIPLE #16 THE BEST DEFENSE

> *"Hitting the other guy before he hits you is the best kind of defense."*
> -Ramsey Dewey

Self protection application

The BEST defense is a good offense.

If you have no other choice but to fight to defend your life or the life of someone else, you must "go first". You must go animal and attack attack attack. You must switch the paradigm from being the prey to becoming the predator. Be first. Be ferocious.

> *"Success in war depends on the "golden rules of war": Speed, simplicity, and boldness."*
> -General George Patton

Leadership application

As a leader, you must do everything you can to stay in "Attack Mode".

People expect their leaders to be able to "wage war". They want their leaders to have the brains and the backbone to be capable of protecting them and winning.

Attack Mode is offensive and proactive. Defend Mode is defensive and reactive.

PRINCIPLE #17 THE WATER BALLOON AND THE ICE SCULPTURE (BE LIKE WATER)

> *"Be like water making its way through cracks. Do not be assertive, but adjust to the object, and you shall find a way around or through it. If nothing within you stays rigid, outward things will disclose themselves. Empty your mind, be formless. Shapeless, like water. If you put water into a cup, it becomes the cup. You put water into a bottle and it becomes the bottle. You put it in a teapot, it becomes the teapot. Now, water can flow or it can crash. Be water, my friend."*
> -Bruce Lee

Self protection application

In fighting, sometimes you need to be fluid like a water balloon. Other times you need to be solid like the ice sculpture. Combatives are a continuous cycling of relaxation and explosion (tension), over and over again.

A counterintuitive secret of martial arts: the majority of time, you are relaxed and fluid like the water balloon.

> *"I'm to the point now where if I get negativity from someone, I don't even respond back."*
> -Andy Frisella

Leadership application

As a leader, you want to develop a "multi-dimensional personality".

You want to be able to stay calm during tense or crisis situations. The calmest one in the room is usually in the most control of any situation.

Warren Buffett on emotional control:

"You will continue to suffer if you have an emotional reaction to everything that is said to you.

True power is sitting back and observing things with logic.

True power is restraint.

If words control you, that means everyone else can control you.

Breathe and allow things to pass."

The other side of your multi-dimensional personality is the ability to be honest and direct and challenge others to be better when necessary.

PRINCIPLE #18 SPLATTER FACTOR

> *"Techniques fail. Focus on principles and keep going!"*
> -Sal Mascoli, ret. United States Marine and law enforcement officer

Self protection application

Real fights are not smooth and sequential and clean like you see in the movies. They are messy, dirty, and scary. This is the "Splatter Factor". There are no foolproof, 100% "guaranteed to work" techniques. The most important thing is that you keep going, keep moving, and keep fighting until you've given every last ounce of your energy and breath.

Because of the unpredictability and chaos of the fight, we want to focus on principles over techniques.

> *"It's better to be in motion ignorantly than static intelligently. Ignorance on fire is better than knowledge on ice."*
> -Sean Smith

Leadership application

Done is better than perfect. Sometimes good enough is good enough. Progress over perfection. Once you have 80% of the information, make a decision and go. Don't overthink this. It's not that complicated.

PRINCIPLE #19 NO GUARANTEES

> *"Techniques fail. Principles don't fail. Keep things simple."*
> *-Jim Grover*

Self protection application

There are no guarantees in self protection situations. No matter how strong, fit, and well trained you are, there are no guarantees that you will defeat your attacker. There are simply too many variables.

Does the attacker have a weapon?

Is your attacker better trained than you?

Does he have accomplices waiting in the shadows to sneak up behind you?

Do you slip on the terrain and injure yourself?

Do you you injure yourself in the initial flurry of the fight?

Do you win the fight, but by doing so face serious legal or financial consequences in the aftermath?

Etc.

There is only one guaranteed technique in combatives: Distance. Don't be there in the first place.

> *"I did one thing to be number one in my market as a vice president at 25 years old. I recruited better. I brought more people into the firm that succeeded than anyone else. Everything else about the job I didn't care about."*
> *-Gary Keller*

Leadership application

There are no guarantees in business or life. It doesn't matter how great your product is or how hard you work. There are no guarantees for success. There are simply too many variables.

PRINCIPLE #20 KEEP SHOWING UP (KEEP TRAINING)

"Nobody cares. Work harder. Keep hammering."
-Cameron Hanes

Self protection application

If you want to put yourself in the best position to be able to defend your life or the lives of people you care about the most, you have to keep showing up.

Showing up where?

To the gym.

Why?

To get comfortable with being uncomfortable.

A life or death struggle is the most uncomfortable thing imaginable.

But if you make yourself uncomfortable every day, you'll be much more comfortable with discomfort if a terrible violent situation ever arises.

"Here's to those unknown and thankless hours, days, months and years of lonely hardship. What you do onstage belongs to the world; but those countless hours of unwitnessed and unappreciated preparation are yours and yours alone. They, not the stage, represent your true character."
-John Danaher

Leadership application

As a leader, you must keep showing up. There are no days off. You must be able to not just show up, but to show up with energy and enthusiasm. Especially on the days you don't feel like it.

One of the absolute true tests of a leader: Can you energize your team even when you don't feel like it?

PRINCIPLE #21 IRON SHARPENS IRON (FIND THE BEST PEOPLE)

> *"You are the average of the five people you spend the most time with. Show me your friends and I'll show you your future."*
> *-Jim Rohn*

Self protection application

Surround yourself with the best and brightest.

In martial arts training, your coaching and training partners are very important. Iron sharpens iron. It is crucial to have great people around you to make you better.

The best investment you can ever make is in yourself. The more you invest in yourself, the more you can help others. Hire the best martial arts coaches and strength and conditioning trainers that you CANNOT afford. That means that you may have to sacrifice in other areas of your life and the things that you spend money on.

> *"Who you are is who you attract. That is the law of magnetism. If you want to attract better people, become the kind of person you desire to attract."*
> *-John C. Maxwell*

Leadership application

As a leader, you must be the kind of person you want to attract onto your team and into your organization.

If you want to attract positive team members, you must be positive.

If you want to attract focused team members, you must be focused. If you want to attract energized team members, you must be energized.

And if you want to attract high integrity team members, you must be high integrity.

PRINCIPLE #22 TEN MINUTES WITH A MENTOR (FIND THE BEST COACHES)

> *"You can't be what you can't see. You must get exposed to the quality you want to have."*
> *-Jay Shetty*

Self protection application

Ten minutes with a world class mentor or coach can be worth more than ten years with good instructor.

You'll learn more spending time with a world class mentor or coach than you will reading 100 books.

Surround yourself with the best mentors and coaches you possibly can. It is one of the only true shortcuts to success, and it is by far the most powerful.

> *"The best piece of advice I ever received: Ignore 99 out of 100 people. But when you find that 1 person, listen to everything they say."*
> *-Tai Lopez*

Leadership application

Show me your heroes, I'll show you your future.

Who are your leadership heroes?

Read their books and biographies. Listen to their interviews and speeches. And if possible, meet them in person.

Spend as much time as possible with people who are five to fifty years ahead of you at where you want to be. If you ask, they'll tell you exactly what you need to do, and equally as important, they'll tell you exactly what not to waste your time on.

PRINCIPLE #23 WEAPONIZE YOUR INSTINCTS

> *"Caveman Vs Scientist: Sometimes you have to be a scientist and sit back and think, and sometimes you have to be a caveman, bite down on your mouthpiece, and outwill the other person."*
> *-Daniel Bohigian, Brazilian Jiu Jitsu Black Belt*

Self protection application

In the initial physical flurry and tornado of a violent situation where you must defend yourself, I can promise you that there is not much thinking going on.

You will go on autopilot, and four things will come out:

1. The simple techniques that you've trained
2. Gross motor skills
3. Your primal inclinations and natural tendencies
4. Your strength and fitness

> *"A billionaire appears to be someone who is a master at everything. But, in truth, they're specialists in one or a few areas and average or subpar at everything else. So, how do they get so much done? Leverage! They do what they do best and get others to do the rest."*
> *-Paul C. Brunson*

Leadership application

Figure out what your biggest strengths are as a leader. Examples:

Public speaking

One-on-one conversations

Media relations

Writing

Reading and researching

Energizing the team by walking around and talking to small groups and individuals

Sales

Marketing

Finance

Product development

Customer service

Strategy

Narrow it down to your two biggest strengths, and double down on them.

Match them up with the two vital functions of the organization, the two things that drive results the most, and you will have mega-success.

PRINCIPLE #24 WHITE BELT MENTALITY (NEVER STOP LEARNING)

> *"I always knew I'd be successful because I knew I worked harder than anyone else. What I lacked in talent, I'd make up for with tenacity and learning."*
> *-Criss Angel*

Self protection application

No matter how much experience and knowledge you have, always show up with a willingness to listen and learn.
A White Belt Mentality is having a "beginners mind".
There is always more to learn if you keep your mind open.

> *"One hour per day of study will put you at the top of your field within three years. Within five years you'll be a national authority. In seven years, you can be one of the best people in the world at what you do."*
> *-Earl Nightingale*

Leadership application

Out of the 500-plus leadership principles, habits, and tactics that I know, continuous learning is in the top-five highest impact of them all.
Leaders are learners.
Leaders are readers.
And knowledge is the biggest competitor advantage.

Recommended Books, Films and Documentaries, and YouTube Channels

Combatives Books

Combatives for Street Survival by Kelly McCann

The Fence by Geoff Thompson

Complete Book of Urban Combatives by Lee Morrison

When Violence Is The Answer by Tim Larkin

The Gift of Fear by Gavin de Becker

Protecting the Gift by Gavin de Becker

Strength and Conditioning books

The New Rules Of Lifting by Alwyn Cosgrove

Maximum Strength by Eric Cressey

5/3/1 by Jim Wendler

100 Strength Training Tips For Combat Athletes by Brooks Kubik

The Ultimate Leaders Library

The Success Principles 10th Anniversary edition by Jack Canfield

The 50th Law by Robert Greene

Unreasonable Success And How To Achieve It by Richard Koch

You Squared and The Quantum Leap Strategy by Dr. Price Pritchett

Tools of Titans by Tim Ferriss

The Charisma Myth by Olivia Fox Cabane

Great Leaders Have No Rules by Kevin Kruse

Talking The Winner's Way (How To Talk to Anyone) by Leil Lowndes

Essentialism by Greg McKeown

One Thing by Gary Keller

15 Secrets Successful People Know About Time Management by Kevin Kruse

The 150 Most Effective Ways to Boost Your Energy by Jonny Bowden

No B.S. Time Management by Dan Kennedy

The Crystal Magnates by Truman Alexander

Awesomely Simple by John Spence

The Score Takes Care of Itself by Bill Walsh

The Culture Code, Daniel Coyle

The Go-Giver by Bob Burg

The 21 Irrefutable Laws of Leadership by John C. Maxwell

Film and Documentary
Fightville documentary

Legendary Nights: Gatti Vs Ward (HBO)

Gatti Vs Ward (boxing trilogy)

Westside Vs The World documentary

Dragon: The Bruce Lee Story (Jason Scott Lee)

The Last Samurai (Tom Cruise)

Warrior (Tom Hardy)

Outstanding Combatives YouTube Channels

Urban Combatives (Lee Morrison)

Urban Combatives Netherlands

Kembativz Brand (Kelly McCann)

Hard2Hurt (Icy Mike)

Mick Coup

Nick Drossos Defense Tactics

Stephan Kesting

Fight SCIENCE

Gracie Breakdown

Samir Seif

Fit To Fight Republic

Shivworks

Aperture Fight Focused

Vee AJ JuJitsu

Sheepdog Response (Tim Kennedy)

Active Self Protection

Funker Tactical Fight Training

Outstanding science-based strength and conditioning YouTube channels

The Bioneer

AthleanX

Jeff Nippard

Jeremy Ethier

Bob and Brad (Physical Therapists)

Outstanding Peak-Performance YouTube Channels

Evan Carmichael Top 10 Rules For Success

Optimize channel PNTV book summaries by Brian Johnson

BestBookBits

The Charisma Matrix by Barron Cruz

Dillon Freed

Basketball Brain

What You Will Learn

Clark Kegley

Joseph Rodrigues

Lewis Howes School of Greatness

The Tim Ferriss Show

Tom Bilyeu

James Altucher

Mindsmash

MyComeUp

Charisma On Command

Vanessa Van Edwards

The Life Coach School with Brooke Castillo

Aaron Doughty

The Swedish Investor

About The Author

A.J. Madden is a peak-performance coach and author based out of Bellefonte, Pennsylvania. He has a Bachelor of Arts degree in Philosophy from Bloomsburg University.

A.J. has spent the last 20 years studying and teaching the psychology and habits of high performance.

He works with individuals and organizations who are in the top 1% in the of their field (or are trying to get there).

All of his clients are ACE's:

Astronomical goals

Clear integrity

Extremely committed

A.J. has coached organizations in 57 different categories in 8 states and 3 countries. He has advised 34 female business owners and leaders. He has spent the last 20 years helping to build and improve businesses and organizations.

His mission is simple:

1. Help high-performance, high-impact individuals and organizations achieve their number-one most important goal and best share their special gifts with the world
2. To improve individual and organizational performance any time, any place
3. To remove any obstacles and friction holding you back from unleashing your full and unlimited potential

4. To help people go from great to greater and get to the next level (because even the best can get better)

A.J. donates a portion of every client's fees to help feed underprivileged individuals and families.

You can find more information about his coaching for individuals and organizations at coachajmadden.com.

www.ingramcontent.com/pod-product-compliance
Lightning Source LLC
Chambersburg PA
CBHW070636220526
45466CB00001B/194